THIS MUST BE WHERE MY OBSESSION WITH INFINITY BEGAN

essays

Joe Bonomo

ORPHAN PRESS

Copyright © 2013 by Joe Bonomo

All rights reserved.

This book or any portion thereof may not be reproduced or used in any manner whatsoever without the express written permission of the publisher except for the use of brief quotations in a book review.

Printed in the United States of America

First Printing 2013

ISBN 978-0-615-75545-8

Orphan Press
8949 Rowley Cove
Cordova, TN 38016

Book & cover design: Greg Larson
Editor: Kristen Iversen

Printed in the United States of America

www.orphanpress.com

For my family

There is no such things as *was*—only *is*.
 — William Faulkner

An idea is salvation by imagination.
 — Frank Lloyd Wright

Thanks to the editors who first published these pieces, and to my students, colleagues, and friends for the many lively, valuable conversations down the years. Thanks to Kristen Iversen, Greg Larson, and everyone at Orphan Press. Special thanks and love to Amy.

This Must Be Where My Obsession With Infinity Began

Contents

Exegesis   15

Mass Of Space

Drafting the Beast   19
Lime Green   23
After Serving   29
Throwing Stones at Mina   31
Swooning at Saint Andrew's   35
This Exhalation   39
After Cornell   41
One Halloween   49
Looking for Karl   51
The Magicians   65

Margins Of The Body

The Blur Family   69
Spying on the Petries   73
Acting Lessons   81
Bob's Blues   83
On Gazing   93
9th Street   103
Caught   105
Cathy or Katy   127

Length And Breadth

Colonizing the Past	133
Stories	137
Trains and Ties	139
Suburban Abstract	151
Fragments of Terrain	153
Forts	161
Transparencies	163
The Apple Carved	167
There Was the Occasional Disruption	173
Student Killed by Freight Train	177
Yard Trauma	187

God-Blurred World

The Innocents	191
Abstracting My Dad	193
The Sky's Tent	197
Customized Environmental Sound Machine	205
The God-Blurred World	207
Occasional Prayer	219
The Alphabet in the Shag Carpet	229
Into the Fable	233
Gone	235
Acknowledgements	247

Exegesis

1. in cleavage and fear of the dark of the second-grade school desk rests his mother's photograph 2. loss, perfume of soft Saturday evenings, mouth moist with attended love 3. and a voice a soprano note held and yearning to slip into palms, pulse next to him in pew 4. in pew her voice ringing down the spine welling its drift from a choir loft 5. or, climbing the stairs clutching her side for cramps she feels the months fall and rest to be studied in the bathroom light 6. there's drama played out in the strain in passion he can't see 7. indifference to the weight of groceries lifted in each Saturday hands numb from lifting, listing 8. small drama of frozen foods, odor of onions in brown paper bags—small gratitudes in mesh—the cans and cans of Cragmont cola— 9. there's a resistant tendon 10. an arthritic shoulder howls beneath his touch 11. my mother told me a story

This Must Be Where My Obsession With Infinity Began

Mass of Space

This Must Be Where My Obsession With Infinity Began

Drafting the Beast

In a backyard in Wheaton, Maryland, I thrust my hand into some sand. I lift out my hand, fingers-splayed. Delicate as powder. A silt of the imagination lingers on skin stretched over bone, a ramshackle draft of an x-ray machine: how bone appears. Late morning splinters all around this discovery.

Later, the sun moving its moist palm over town, the earth recoiling, I'll draw an outline of my outstretched hand on loose leaf paper, draw with black ink in ice-conditioned air a slow line around thumb, index finger, middle finger, all the way around back to wrist.

Aren't we always drafting the beast inside? I repeat this to myself that night in the darkness of my bedroom, my brother breathing the contours of his body out and breathing his body back next to me—while under cover of some sort of progress I grip my finger and press the tip of the nail down into flesh as the nail whitens, again, and once again the body's secret is released as light.

When the Air and Space Museum opened on the Mall in Washington D.C., my excited dad—an IBM engineer who worked with NASA, a mathematics devotee—brought the family in from Wheaton to visit. The photos he or my mom snapped that day are oddly, brutally under-lit—the result of the dim interior lighting at the museum, possibly, or a camera snafu. The haze which permeates the photos feels retroactively appropriate decades later, not only as a visual equivalent to the gauzy curtain of memory and a vanished childhood but because I experienced something that afternoon that complicated things.

Among the exhibits at the museum was Ray and Charles Eames' nine-minute documentary *Powers of Ten*, a film that explores the relative scale of the universe by journeying across it in powers of ten, moving outward from earth to the edges of the galaxy, and then back, into and through the human body. As I remember, the film ran on a loop at a small, wood-paneled kiosk outside one of the main exhibit halls on an upstairs floor. Wandering around, probably on my own, I came across the display and took note of a small, obviously interested crowd gathered; weaseling my way in among grown-ups, I started watching. What I saw captivated me immediately: the narrator's voice was dry but friendly, not intimidating or pedantic, and at the point where I started watching the film we seemed to be out in the cosmos somewhere. Cool!—but soon vaguely unsettling, and then weird, and then amazing, and then scary. I stood for what felt like an hour watching, hooked on the trip from a Chicago couple dozing on the grass near Lake Michigan out to the infinite reaches of space. The video reversed back to earth, then into and under the surface of the man's hand, probing relentlessly toward his basic cellular makeup, the randomness of protons madly humming and humping and colliding and reacting, an unreal but obvious universe inside my own body. Struck,

Drafting the Beast

I watched the loop again and again, quietly disappearing, a kind of cosmic journey that tattooed me.

There it was, proof that the inside of the human body was chaotic, patterned, and maybe endless. I stared down at my hand, imagining the dark inside. It was overwhelming to consider the molecular makeup of the body, that things I couldn't see inside of me were reacting and going on all over the place, buzzing, storming, colliding. I entwined the parallel images of the dark of outer space and the dark inside my body without understanding the science. The film was mostly beyond me, though I don't recall being bored. Something struck a chord in my imagination: the body is an imitation of the universe. It was heady stuff, half-understood, shelved away once I reunited with my family and we departed, visiting other museums, and then left the city. I returned to nearby suburbia, to girls, to Saint Andrew the Apostle, bike-riding, and the Beatles, my backyard, all things infinitely small and infinitely large.

This Must Be Where My Obsession With Infinity Began

Lime Green

The sudden shift from black & white to Technicolor in the opening third of *The Wizard of Oz* was the most dramatic juxtaposition of textures and worlds possible. I thought this, until a moment when I was ten.

The required uniform for girls at Saint Andrew the Apostle consisted of a plain white buttoned blouse, a knee-length black-and-white plaid skirt, white socks, and black dress shoes. *School noir.* When Susan strutted into our fourth-grade classroom swinging her bantam hips and dancing the end of her tongue over lip-glossed lips, she quickly sized up the situation: a dozen gawking boys. She pulled the hem of her regulation skirt with both hands and in a flash yanked it up and let it drop. A diamond of bright lime green underwear winked in the sunlight through the window, in an instant, and was gone. Her skirt settled like a bed sheet, and rested.

Mr. Ossi labored, but such absolute physics could not be reconstructed in science class.

Under wraps. The eight years I spent in Catholic grade school resolve themselves, as does any chunk of time, into potent

This Must Be Where My Obsession With Infinity Began

imagery: certainly, the Stations of the Cross, sun-drenched, encumbered narratives; and the immense shadow-continent of the hanging cross above the altar; the intimate and secretive sacristy, hushed with so much cloaked anxiety. The steeple against a beige, unhappy sky.

Rob and Andy pawing through the plastic bag of pre-Consecration communion wafers during recess, stuffing pale discs into their mouths as so many Fritos, damned giggles and crumbs everywhere; Vanessa flopping herself into her desk chair and splaying her legs wide open, announcing "I don't believe in God," being implored to sit like a lady, not an elephant; and, after she fainted, Catherine's head slamming into the pew, a queer smile on her pale face.

The original Latin usage of *obsession* suggested the ruling of the corporeal body—helpless infant—by an evil spirit. Once, Sister Nena tripped over the rug in our fourth-grade classroom and fell to the floor very hard, then stood hopelessly idle and flushed while her thick, pious-brown skirt rode up her leg, revealing considerable forbidden thigh; Danny—who surely was shaving by this point, daily—discretely offered to rearrange the Sister, to smooth out the awkward fabric. She demurred, and we were to believe the moment annulled. Our own growing legs on which we walked home from school, sometimes together, disappeared—no, were abolished, brought to nothing—beneath the vaulted roof of Sister Nena's skirt. Pillars to, belief in, something bigger. *Faith,* Hebrews instructs, *the evidence of things not seen.*

The body evaporated into thin air a lot in Catholic school. During the Eucharist, at the moment of Consecration, Father Krastel held the wafer and then the wine to the heavens, to the ceiling, and I was trained to utter *My Lord and My God* under my breath, a delicate *sotto voce;* failing to do so would result not in a botched sacrament, a communal embarrassment, but a missed miracle, or a missed opportunity for some proof, some action: a photo-op. But as earnestly as I strained my eyes, there were no transubstantiated visions. No video. What begins in origin as a kind of transparent faith, remains.

As altar boys, our bodies disappeared under our vestments: in Spring, during Lent, limbs moved invisibly under ghost-white, the body fasting into oblivion. Sunday mornings when we were late and sleepless, we hurried to pull from the sacristy closet a robe that fit, often failing, loafers or tattered sneakers peeping out from below our hems, two feet in this world. The priests were all large, dense men. Bodies. They'd sometimes throw all their weight behind slamming a shelf door in the sacristy if things weren't operating smoothly.

Soon, and after not a little controversy, the girls joined, became altar servers, pulled by decree their lovely blonde or walnut hair into tight buns, nascent curves and ripeness vanishing beneath cloaks. They seemed very serious.

What do priests wear under there?

I had a gargantuan, colossal, goliath crush on Susan, who would never have been an altar server—and to my complete luck she lived near me, at the top of the hill on Arcola Avenue, around the corner from the end of my street; we walked home together after school nearly everyday. The blush of nostalgia: Susan's fig mouth; when she smiled it flowered, a violet with moist white teeth, playful little tongue. She had a diamond-shaped face to match, ringed with waves of dirty-blonde hair. Everything on her sparkled. Everything on me trembled.

This is at least how I remember her. Sometimes she'd wait for me across the street from Saint Andrew's, at the intersection of Arcola and Kemp Mill—actually wait for me; I hadn't known a girl could behave like a friend. My heart would pound up through my throat when I reached her; I felt envied, unique. She swung her books, but I was too frightened, cautious, to suggest I hold them for her on our walk home.

Clarity and blur. Whatever version of Susan I experienced, I conjured up, we truly were friends, as I struggle to recall, and our walks home were filled with squeals of laughter and innocent chasing, hijinx of the purest kind. When we'd reach her house each day I couldn't help but take note—in the somewhat fearful manner that children do—of her house; plainly, it was shabby: younger siblings peered from windows wearing nothing, and Susan's mom appeared, in my ten-year old perspective, outlaw-ish, hippy-ish. Susan's father was never to be found, and the ramifications of that observation soon burned up the playground.

None of this mattered much because Susan continued to smile at me. And she smiled at many other boys. Several years later during high school, when I thought I saw Susan push an infant baby in a stroller past my house—she'd left Saint Andrew's and attended public grammar and high schools and as far as I was concerned vanished into thin air, though she still lived in the neighborhood—I thought back to the morning she lifted her skirt and flashed us her lime green panties. She broke rules, I followed them. My loss and confusion never found a voice.

Susan's brazenness hoisted a doomed (if melodramatic) cleavage on our friendship-crush: but my confusion at the thrill I experienced that moment was predicated less on some childish cry of betrayal then on simple, overpowering hormones, though the hoots and whistles from my classmates rang ugly in my ears; it was as if they were suddenly speaking in tongues, locking me out. Jarring: Susan's impudent flash cast an unalterable power over me, over all of us boys, over the daily lessons. I struggled longingly, excitedly, to witness a physical transformation at the altar; I listened with all my body, for body. How sadly dismissive we were with faith, with simple faith, at the sight of Susan's underneaths.

This Must Be Where My Obsession With Infinity Began

After Serving

I stuff my cassock in a closet. I dream of the Washington Redskins. I dream of Jenny and Wendy in pink underwear. I dream of an Italian sub. I dream of launching myself into the woods. I dream of bleeding sunlight. I dream of incense drifting into neglected corners. I dream of incense in haze. I dream loudly, as after silence. I dream of stink. I dream of counting sleepless heads in vapor. I dream of the change beneath my bed, and of transubstantiation. I dream of magic tricks evaporating, offered up into a noon sky. I dream of driving someday. I dream of the smell of ash wood, of the muddy field. I dream that the sun will continue its slow demise, someday giving up the far, pinched cry of the smothered baby. I dream of offering, of prayer, of social studies. I dream of the large, chapped fingers of the man whose hands I wash. I dream of the evacuated body. I dream of the altar. A sacristy is a room in a church. A cassock gropes emptily in a dark closet.

This Must Be Where My Obsession With Infinity Began

Throwing Stones at Mina

When Jenny fought Wendy and Jackie and Tracy on the playground steps at Saint Andrew the Apostle, it was the end of the Seventies and America had citizens held hostage in Iran. *Mina, a round, dark girl of Iranian descent, and Natalia, yet another unpopular girl, wait at the fringe.*

Minutes prior to the girl-fight a few of us poked fun at President Carter's botched rescue attempt—could we have we learned of it that very morning?—it seemed to us inept, embarrassing. It was cold out, we were soon to be let in from recess, and abruptly, at the front of the line: high-pitched shrieks, hair flying, uniform dresses yanked up, white and light-green cotton panties. Monday, I'd nonchalantly spied as Jenny made brave gestures toward Mina and Natalia at the swing set; soon Jenny was swinging and squealing with flying hair, but this was junior high now and they had to muscle the small children from their rightful places. Had it been a few months earlier, when Jenny was a popular girl, she wouldn't have been near the swings, *or in my daydream her saffron wind of hair streaming like a waterfall as the swing arched.* But Jenny had inexplicably cut her hair from long to Dorothy

31

Hamill—she once told me that she washed her hair twice, sometimes three times a day, and I felt lucky to know—and the day she arrived at school with her hair cut short, prideful and fearful, was the day she began to lose her popularity or, in pre-teen parameters, herself. Now on Friday she's swinging with Mina and Natalia: something strange to the surface of our teenage lives.

And now they're fighting, and it's awful, because Wendy and Jackie and Tracy are ganging up on Jenny and everyone's pulling hair and it sounds like the yanking off of limbs and when all of them are crying and screeching it sounds hellish. Faces are flush and ashamed, very, very knowing: glimpses into far-away, candid distress, and behind eyes fear usually left in the bedroom. The bell rings at some point and the fight ends, Jenny never gets any closer to Wendy or Jackie or Tracy, later she moves to Texas and elopes. She's pregnant by high school. I don't know whatever became of Wendy or Jackie or Tracy, the popular girls.

Mina and Natalia watch. And that's about it.

When the memory of earth particulars fades, what's left: the smell of loam, the anguish of tongue in the dirt. Tess Gallagher wrote that the poet is the enemy of the photograph, when in fact the sensory snapshot, the lone, long image flickering in the shadow, may be the only true ally. Maybe I lied, but only to get at the truth: it was Jenny, she was maybe fighting one girl. Where's the script? Were I to trek to the local library, eighth-grade class photo in hand, I might discover via the sobering veracity of microfilm that there could be no intersection of Carter's attempted, aborted rescue attempt and my feeble memory, that what feels like months was in fact days, or maybe hours. The disposition of memory, the half-snatched snippet of song, end-strands waving wildly into the dark: who knows where you pick it up, but that it taps you now. The resonance of pugilism and of calendar truth: foreign currency exchange, one for the other? And where was I? Inside, outside, nowhere to be seen?

Mina, a round, dark girl of Iranian descent, and Natalia, yet another unpopular girl, wait at the fringe. Who knows the parameters of that fringe, whether such geometric truths really matter: were they there? They were somehow witnesses, their new friend Jenny, formerly popular, flayed publicly for her innocence, themselves to blame. Were they even in my grade?

The stones flew with about as much accuracy as our footballs and our dodgeballs. The vernacular of shame enters young minds as pine and as blacktop, with the most innocent of origins. When some kid (Mike? Andy? Rob?) started chasing my best friend Paul, throwing gravel and clumps of sod, yelling after him "Jew! Jew!!", they chose up sides in the usual manner, feeling both theatrics and shame. We knew that Paul couldn't be a Jew; though we barely knew what a Jew was, we knew that we were Catholics, this was ridiculous. But they chased and scorned, and Paul's bewildered face grew red and complicated. The bell rang, and the next day it either continued or it ended, I can't remember.

Mina and Natalia near the swing set, yelling back, smiling, throwing handfuls of small parking-lot pebbles, heaving, and red. We threw with glee and determination, without motive. Green rhetoric. Try as I might to remember otherwise, now into the classroom I go where I and several others are being lectured solemnly. We have been caught throwing stones at

This Must Be Where My Obsession With Infinity Began

Mina, and I listen to the defense with a hollow chest, with machismo.

The older one grows, the smaller percentage of life one's childhood becomes. This much I can prove: the hostages were soon freed and President Reagan stepped in. I hadn't thrown stones at Mina. Maybe a friend grabbed me as he was being hauled in to be reprimanded, fingered me as an accomplice. Where affinity mingles with guilt, memory stalls and reconstructs, on its own, stern lies and chivalrous truths, the life we live in the next minute.

Swooning at Saint Andrew's

When Catherine's head hit the pew we all looked around startled, the silence shattered, as if somebody had dropped something they were holding. We felt the dull *thud* at the backs of our necks and heads. The grave presence of something having fallen.

It's not an accident that we acknowledge two definitions of the act of *swooning*: to lose consciousness, and to experience rapturous emotion. These two qualities live side by side in the person who has fainted: the very life-breath is taken away, and at once passion swells as if from the lungs of God. Catherine was a doughy girl, not at all popular. I struggle to reassemble her image in my mind: pale blue eyes; a plump, oval head; freckles; frizzy hair; thick ankles. My inventory suggests not a girl but a type, and that's now how she lives in my memory, as a type of person in the long, blurred line of the myth-journey. "I am inclined to believe that God's chief purpose in giving us memory," Frederick Buechner observes, "is to enable us to go back in time so that if we didn't play those roles right the first time around, we can still have another go at it now." Catherine is one of the girls from my past who I wouldn't recognize now. Why, then, do I feel compelled to reach out to her, if only through memory's stubborn attempt at rehabilitation? I wasn't friends with her in grade school; I wasn't friends with her friends. Yet her image plagues me, haunts my memory in a kind of instruction.

When Catherine fainted in church it was during the most pedestrian of services, daily Mass, the rare respite from the dim classroom and hallways. It was the afternoon, if I am to trust the pale, warm sun leaning in through the high church windows. We were gathered together in our plaid school uniforms in a small section of the church; perhaps it was only a few grades at Mass that day. Catherine was behind me, and slightly to my right. At what point in the mass she fell I don't remember. The thud of body hitting the wood could have come at any time though I suspect it was late in the service, the mustiness of the church having finally confounded her small body. Any specific memories I have cannot be respected, as before this moment there was nothing out of the ordinary about the day. I might even have my age wrong, the time of the day wrong, though I know I did not dream the afternoon, as the physical presence of Catherine has settled into my marrow in a way that dreams never can, pretenders to life's sinew.

The sound of her body dropping was shocking, especially so in a hushed building where sound tolls only on the soundtrack of your own faith, the music of wanting to believe. The few post-collapse cries and gasps of my fellow classmates and of the teachers in the moments after she fainted underscored the drama, but they were superfluous, really: the theatrics for me were staged the moment Catherine's soft head slammed into the pew, one of the moments during my adolescent years in church when body became body, when we were reminded

Swooning at St. Andrew's

of our slimmest faiths, and our greatest vulnerabilities.

Every memory we have ever had which lingers in us as fable begs to be understood as contents for a larger content. Why do I recall the following images from my childhood, two grainy frames: *in front of class, Danny gently smoothing Sister Nena's skirt after she'd fallen; Susan chewing her gum and undoing a button on her white uniform blouse*. Two tiny tales, their larger narratives slow in catching up to them. Both Danny's and Susan's versions of *body* were innocent: one boy trusted the body's language, one girl trusted the body's language. It wasn't until much later that we could sort out the different wisdoms embodied in those gestures. What we assemble, memory by memory, arches from a kind of craving, to a kind of knowledge.

"God utters me like a word containing a partial thought of Himself. A word will never be able to comprehend the voice that utters it," observes Thomas Merton. This is colossal thinking. Since the day Catherine passed out in church I've wondered whether I, too, didn't fall.

Perhaps Catherine fainted because she was a young girl who hadn't eaten well that morning or who had difficulties in warm, humid environments or who had a thyroid condition or who was suffering stress from a her parents' bitterness. None of these clinical possibilities, these rationalities, mattered to me at the moment. What mattered was the splash of cold fear in my chest when Catherine went down. Beyond the nervous giggles and squashed laughter of kids, the moment telescoped, and I wonder now if that fear that I experienced wasn't a kind of idiom, a kind of language-knowledge that so tattooed me with lore that I've been struck dumb.

What I've yet to write about is the look on Catherine's

37

face as she was revived. I remember expecting her to be mortified: surely this unfortunate event would only cement her status as the butt of cruel humor and misunderstanding. I remember wanting to look away, but I didn't. Beneath the nuns and a single giving girl waving missalettes and handkerchiefs at Catherine's sweaty face, there beamed from the now-conscious girl a look of simple but absolute contentment, of dazed and absorbed peace, and pleasure. There were no furtive glances toward the popular gallery of girls, no beseeching glances at the faculty, no apologies or hasty smoothing out of a rumpled skirt. Catherine looked so serene as to look post-coital, as if her tiny eleven-year old body had been awash with a desire and a fulfillment so immense that she lay low in a kind of glaze of ecstasy. Her forehead was damp, her cheeks flush.

So, this is why memory lingers. So I might look beyond therapeutic reason toward a larger, irrational desire for Catherine's countenance as a kind of salvation. She fairly floated out of herself, I remember, and the queer expression on her face as she came to was so odd to us kids that it itself became fodder for later, unrelenting teasing and ostracizing, and Catherine disappearing to the corner of the playground. But it also lingered in me as proof of something larger than mere suggestion. It lingers as one body, frightened at the sudden noise that another can make, yearning to understand the language the other body was speaking, as it rose from the pews and lifted its damp arms to receive the futile, mortal gestures of the bodies surrounding it.

This Exhalation

I knew a woman who grew up in a funeral home, knew the moaning and wailing, the dream-like harp during family wakes while she drew or wrote, or tried to sleep, the seep of formaldehyde like plum or pear—air, awakening to its waxed fate, rushing from uncollapsed cavities, the dead body sighing. Sundays in church and the bare loft, long after the choir had left to congregate closer to the altar, sent whispers too mysterious to protest as anything more than wind through pipe, or creaks in floorboards, however this affirmation of silence, this exhalation, came.

This Must Be Where My Obsession With Infinity Began

After Cornell

Really, a grope in the dark is all there is. To recollect the sacrament of penance one first drenches the body in darkness and purifies memory from sentiment and myth—though the act of confessing is imbued with sentiment and myth, especially to the young. Rainer Maria Rilke recalled encountering once, when he was a small child, a disembodied hand while he was momentarily beneath a table; in the darkness the extremity surprised him in its disassociated warmth and comfort, though he could not tell in the intervening moments whose hand it was—his, or his housekeeper's?

One always hoped for existential discoveries in the confessional box, that the body still did exist, that one hadn't left entirely. Succor was sometimes delivered in the reassuring tones of the priest's voice, a timbre recollected from last week's classroom visit; sometimes it was one's tired knees, or trembling elbows. One needed to depart from the corpus if one was to truly confess.

This, I believed, was why I wasn't allowed to see the priest's face when I confessed: to stare eye-to-eye when confessing belied the obvious, *I am flesh-and-blood, I am less-than-whole.* To comprehend moral and ethical transgressions—regardless of how domestically petty they might feel to the confessor *(last night dear Lord I bit my little brother)*—the confessor must shed anatomy's garment and step in unencumbered. The reminder that we are always flesh filtered through the shadowy screen between priest and penitent, and such a reminder could not have been allowed to distract.

But spiritual grace was impossible in the confessional. The body was always interrupting, one's voice welling from a palpitating source more physical than celestial, perspiring than divine. The body struggling in the dark in a kind of dramatic nobility, the body enclosed in the small, enormous dark box behind the plum-velvet curtain where whispers strayed like incense, and where the body threatened to dissipate. But always we returned to the world with the body intact. Always we returned to the confessional with the body in disarray.

Smaller enormities. An untitled Joseph Cornell construction circa 1969, known familiarly as "For Trista," dramatizes the geometric intrigue implicit in all boxes and, as with all of Cornell's creations, that which is left out—that which is imagined—moves invisibly within and without as contents for the content. "For Trista" consists of a 14-by-18-by-5 inch upright wooden box; dropped in snugly, nearly at box's depth, is a pale, thin piece of plywood with a one and-a-half inch hole excised just off-center. *Peering through* is the operative behavior when encountering a Cornell box: through this hole one spies a dim detail of an archaic, other-century map (when the panel is removed, the map is revealed to be a chart of "Principal Rivers"). In the box's lower-right hand corner, lying simply and innocently in front of the plywood sheet as if on a ledge: a single maroon wooden bead; a blue cube; a plastic globe. (My description is based on the physical arrangement of materials organized by the curators at the Art Institute in Chicago, where the construction is on permanent display. The piece achieves its fullest dimension with the panel installed, and with the globe—which in other installations is propped inside the panel-hole—resting at the base alongside the bead and cube.) We're reminded that simplicity is made of complex absences.

The word *confessional* comes to us from the French language where it meant, originally, "chair."
    Perhaps this is what the clergy and faculty at St. Andrew the Apostle School had in the back of their minds when during my years in junior high school the sacrament of confession moved inexplicably from the confessional boxes in church to a casual, windowed office at the back of church, the screened cleavage between penitent and absolver forever banished. This was the end of the Seventies and more and more Catholic parishes were making concerted efforts to "reach out" to the youth and reverse their declining interest in all that was pious; this was not a uniquely late-Twentieth century dilemma for the Catholic Church, as all ages deal with spiritual malaise among the young. I know that at the time my church felt it reasonable to assume that the foreboding with which most children and young adults were gripped when they entered the confessional box might yet be harnessed for spiritual gain, even if the severity of the act itself could be lessened somewhat. This was, after all, during the nascent stages of having lay persons distribute communion, of permitting young girls to move slowly into the ranks of

This Must Be Where My Obsession With Infinity Began

altar servers, of seeing teaching-nuns fairly disappear from the classroom; the world was evolving, and I was in it. Why not move penance to a new venue, without sacrificing any of the sacrament's solemnity?

How "innocently" do the bead, cube, and globe lie there in "For Trista"? Any object conspiring with the imagination to subvert daily logic forfeits any claim to innocence, and haphazard artlessness doesn't exist inside a Cornell box. The maker's painstaking processes are legendary and impressive, and I'm always suspicious of (though intrigued by) Cornell's claims that "random chance" plays such an active role in his box-constructions. A close examination of any piece from his "bird sanctuary" series, for example, reveals an artist's eye-for-detail and an expert, well-earned tone embodied by the lively and resonant possibility of juxtaposed *objets trouvés*; the composition in 1945's "Untitled (The Hotel Eden)" falls nothing short of Velázquez's pictorial ambitions in its scope and determination.

And in Cornell's boxes the dark aura of mystery, and of the imagination's being implicated in that mystery, is by requirement doubled. Intrigued at one point by a closed box—*what looms in there?*—Cornell spent the better part of his life opening the lids, as it were. Thus, what one was doubtless convinced by—the enigma as shut chest—becomes multiplied upon further curiosity. The riddle guessed at beneath the lid, or behind the velvet curtain, was more than anyone bargained for, argues Cornell, and isn't this a spectacular gift?

I was wary about confession in the new arrangement. While the old penance frightened me with the cloaked hush of its dark box, this novel face-to-face design introduced a newer, equally fearful prospect: intimacy—not the vast, sacred intimacy of the box, but bodily intimacy, eye contact, body language, a whole host of threatening physical melodramas naturally loathed by the puberty-aged. Perhaps, I rationalized, this was an opportunity to combat the fear of my vanishing body; if I was made visible to myself, the apprehension might be forever erased. But the prospect of having no barrier separating myself and the priest to whom I would confess my sins seemed impossible to bear, the stripping away not only of a certain dignity, but also of an odd sense of comfort: if made invisible during this most personal of moments, then I and my stain would not be seen. At the very least, to thrust myself, flesh, bones, and pounding blood, toward repenting frailties seemed at odds with the liberating casualness surrounding the church's new policy.

I was relieved, then, when I learned that Father Paul was giving confessions that week. Of all of the priests at St. Andrew's he seemed the calmest and the most genial; he seemed, both in the classroom and out on the playground, to go out of his way to leave behind antiquated notions of the steely, stern, and humorless priest. I was also surprised when I learned that the "open-face confession" (as we thirteen-year-old wags had soon dubbed it) was a choice; one could still enter the box and confess the old-fashioned way if one preferred. But by this point I had steeled myself for a face-to-face spiritual admission. The thought of again stepping into a confessional box *(bright mid-afternoon sunlight, bleed of stained-glass, imperturbable silence, kids' outside cries)* seemed akin to stepping into the Old Age, of black, black, black. I was thoroughly modern now, and proud.

This Must Be Where My Obsession With Infinity Began

Cornell subverts the universal knowledge guaranteed by all maps, whether celestial or Mall of America: *You Are Here*. By foreshortening access to such an absurd degree, the piece brings on a tremendous rush of claustrophobia, as if the world is being pinched down to a dot. The bare plywood offers little relief; it's all that separates us from the world, from *proof that the world exists* as vowed by that most absolute of documents, the map. With our vast perspective rapidly diminishing, what have we left? A bead. A cube. A plastic globe.

A bead, a cube, a plastic globe. Child's playthings? Microcosm? That possibility always lurks inside Cornell's boxes, as the child's imaginative apprehension of her world—not yet filtered through rational, social concerns of property disputes and political boundaries—knows no limits but fear and the compulsion to keep moving forward. Cornell created "For Trista" as a gift for the titular child, a young daughter of some friends; what was she to do with this tiny universe of apprehension? There's something remarkable about the diminutive globe resting beneath the ever-eclipsed map, as if we are at once removed warp-speed from our tiny perspective and thrust out into the cosmos. The comforting proximity to a regional map is distorted by our Atlas-towering over the token globe. As our peep-hole quickly dilates, we become, oddly, giants.

But that bead, and that cube—Cezanne-like geometric takes on what remains. The bead: a bald earth. The cube: a receptacle. As man was busy spending the Sixties perfecting his compulsion to shrink the globe down to something palm-sized and possessed, was Cornell obsessed with the crackle of NASA-speak, with Houston's bizarre dialogues?

After Cornell

As I was ushered into the confessional office Father Paul greeted me warmly from the center of the room, calling me by my first name and motioning me to sit down. I did so, in a plush, stuffed leather chair, placed squarely in front of him. The room was comfortable, with tasteful wood paneling and green plants. What I found most odd wasn't the empathic countenance of the priest before me, bearing as it did no likeness whatsoever to the darkened silhouette I was used to muttering toward in the box, but the light in the room. It gave the office the somewhat ersatz aura of a waiting room, continents and eons away from the darkness of the confessional box. The methods of the sacrament themselves hadn't changed, of course; I asked the Father for his blessing, I informed him as to how long it had been since my last confession—I confessed. He nodded, he listened, he smiled, he counseled, he forgave me, he gave me my penance.

Many of the confessional box mores were gone. Something was strangely off, and I was unprepared for how deflating the experience would be. I wasn't conceding my sins on my knees as had been the custom; rather, I was a casual supplicant, sitting with my legs crossed, as was the Father. We chatted; there was back-and-forth conversing, actual dialogue, none of the weighted, speak-and-hush murmuring of the box. There was direct eye contact, there were mild moments of levity. There was no mystery.

Charles Simic on Cornell: "Vision is his subject. He makes holy icons. He proves that one needs to believe in angels and demons even in a modern world in order to make sense of it."

The mysteries belonging to Cornell's boxes are those belonging to us, but which remain unarticulated. As we enter his boxes we agree to leave something behind, if only to save ourselves. Our penance when we return is to be cursed with the inability to translate what we've seen. From small enclosures one can sense the infinite.

The fact that I recall so little of my face-to-face confessions suggests that there was little in them that I found spiritually compelling. In the effort to modernize, to move from the metaphorical-and-literal darkness of the confessional box to an informal discussion in the light, the archdiocese robbed the sacrament of a great deal of its sacred unknowns. The move from dark unburdening to light acknowledgement seemed reasonable, as a turn away from a Joseph Cornell conundrum feels like a turn toward reason. The language of boxes might always be foreign, but a lifting of the lid and a cocking of the ear to odd, fearful music—however unphraseable—protects and enriches more of the soul than does an emptying of the contents into rational light.

One Halloween

They went trick-or-treating. One boy's costume drifted over him all night, barely touching, some queer idea of himself. Now, so much later, he thinks it either blew away over the rooftops or, more likely, settled into himself, *some queer idea of skin. Don't run ahead* they scolded. But tearing to lift out of himself again of course he ran, the ghost and the goblin shrubbery looming before him.

The winds were biting. Safely ahead of the gullible night he bobbed in the dark when from behind a bush a group of older kids leapt—their faces prowling beneath pulled-down pantyhose. They menaced the silly boy into the ground, scattering hard candies, then were off.

He waited for the world to wearily acknowledge him, an unexceptional dark settling its chill in sympathy. Some porch lights came on, others went off.

This Must Be Where My Obsession With Infinity Began

Looking for Karl

The brain is wider than the sky, Emily Dickinson

What's home? Where'd it go? I often ask myself this, usually in transit. Before I knew her, my wife Amy had moved an astonishing 29 times; eventually she simply stopped unpacking her car. We've since established stability together, though we ourselves have moved thrice and threaten to again. Our vague movement westward—we began in Ohio, and have lurked in northern Illinois for years—suggests a form, some larger design. Even writing this I envision our charted course upon the large map, a cursive destiny one day to be read.

One defines home as a part of character: one part deciding-to-act; one part acting; one part peering gloomily into a befogged yard. We carry the notion of our homes inside of us, balmed within our sorry cages as we bend toward cardboard boxes, those little homes so rudely strewn about our larger ones. Though the phrase *settling down* implies permanence, the gray songbird once settled on the yard alights soon enough. The prepositions of our lives tell: do we live *on* the land, or *in* the land? We instruct ourselves that moving is human nature, that to restlessly seek fuels large ambition. And yet we long to lock the door behind us, to shut off the porch light, *in for the night*. Does the home exist, or do we invent the home? The whistle of the train moving past the end of our yard sounds more and more mournful.

The older one becomes, the smaller percentage of life one's childhood becomes. Staring down the long corridor, the contents of our childhoods collect themselves into a rapidly-diminishing corner. Now, many years later, I struggle to piece together the mornings and the afternoons of my friendship with Karl. Its many images live in me cinematically, looping together beyond any surrealist montage toward a larger narrative. But trying to assemble that friendship decades later is like trying to follow dream's logic, and there are no conjunctions in dreams.

Karl and I were best friends. He lived in the house directly behind mine, in Wheaton. We were the same age, though we didn't attend school together: I went to private; he to public. We were too young to let social parameters define us and what I recall are endless hours in my house and his, lost inside the fanciful games we devised and acted out. One week we were Super Spies, the next week Internationally-renowned Inventors hired surreptitiously by President Nixon to . . . well, invent things. We played with a relatively standard collection of name-brand toys, but what I remember most fondly are the days spent drifting through what our imagination shaped for us. Usually this involved homespun charades, self-invented props. Once we were world-famous Oceanographers (a quirky but powerful passion of mine for some time in gradeschool) and we established an exploratory submarine vessel in the downstairs laundry room. Inexplicably the L-shaped corner room had an aquatic drama inherent in it—maybe because of the laundry machine and its attending hoses, or the water rushing endlessly through the exposed plumbing above our heads.

The detail I remember vividly is the window looking out into the sea. Karl and I found blue transparent-plastic plates (or probably they were lids to something) and scotch-taped them onto the white cinder-block walls of the laundry room, affixed over our own magic-marker drawings of veritable ocean life: colorful, swimming fish; undulating seaweed; overturned shells; a shark lurking in the background. The pressure in my inner ears virtually mounted as I peered out of our imaginative portal, listening longingly for the imagined muted bells and beeps of our submarine gadgetry. Long after our game had bored us, after we had moved on to some other adventure, I kept that plastic taped to the wall, and would now and again go down to the laundry room and, assured that I was alone, stare through the azure onto a verisimilitude of weird power. *Metaphor creates a new reality from which the original appears to be unreal*, Wallace Stevens once wrote. Turning away from that wall toward the inevitable chores of a peevish evening was melancholic, and defeating. Through paper and plastic we circumvented our ordinary place in the world.

And we created a home. The emotional context in which Karl and I played was hearth-like in its warmth and domesticity. Whether at my house or his, we created an endearing and deeply-felt sense of home, of place. I didn't acknowledge at the time that this was wholly an imagined place: an eight-

This Must Be Where My Obsession With Infinity Began

year-old is too busy in wonder to care about the nature of reality. Only the stubborn details of the physical world would remind me. The one evening that I spent sleeping overnight at Karl's house discomfited me with its foreign smells and sounds, a strange father, not my own, in beer and boxer shorts, the novelty of a different larger bed. Unaccustomed to the geometry of Karl's bed I rolled off mid-sleep and landed in a loud disoriented heap on the wooden floor; his parents came leaping in to their son's room but by then I had righted myself and was curled up in a ball under the sheets.

But once we both retreated from the palpable world and explored the home inside our imaginations, we met whole again. Karl and I lived sixty-feet apart, but the horizons were endless when we played together. There was no greater intimacy.

Which was why I was confoundedly bewildered when, one day, it was announced that Karl's family was moving to Illinois. As I recall, he told me the news at the north side of his house, near the fence gate. I remember his moist brown eyes, his round face, that Prince Valiant haircut.

But I wonder if this image of Karl is accurate to the image of the boy who broke the news to me. I've reconstructed this moment many times—after so many years it doesn't matter whether I remember it correctly, whether the snapshot in my head relates at all to the particular memory I describe. What's for certain is that after Karl moved, the minutiae of our friendship began their slow, steady decline, their demarcations softening and drifting toward the haze of the oddest, and the saddest, kind of memory: imagined memory.

The afternoon he moved is awash in blur. I remember the family's orange Pacer, stuffed with belongings, as it pulled out of the driveway. I watched it turn the corner at the end of the cul-de-sac, and I remember fiercely wondering why I wasn't crying, feeling some sort of failure that I wasn't a phony in my prickly self-consciousness. After the car disappeared I ran around his house up the side hill to my own house, fists balled up, chest tight. The rest of that day is lost. I know it was 1974.

What next? Over a quarter century of struggling attempts to reconstruct.

Centuries ago St. Augustine wondered on the essential and unshakable problem of the simple act of remembering:

> The power of the memory is prodigious, my God. It is a vast, immeasurable sanctuary. Who can plumb its depths? And yet it is a faculty of my soul. Although it is part of my nature, I cannot understand all that I am. This means, then, that the mind is too narrow to contain itself entirely. But where is that part of it which it does not itself contain? Is it somewhere outside itself and not within it? How, then, can it be a part of it, if it is not contained in it?

The serene purity of his prose nearly belies the heartache. Earlier in *Confessions* he refers to "the vast cloisters" of his memory, and throughout remains stubbornly at a loss to articulate the immensity of the mind's storehouse, and one senses that his awed reticence both amazed and frustrated him. We all share this. Hundreds of years later, closer to twentieth century thought but far away from its clinical research into memory, Emily Dickinson posited the obvious, and the brilliant, complication of recollecting: *the brain is wider than the sky.* The president of Amherst College at the time declared such pronouncements "disastrous to religion." We declare it a salvation, those of us plagued.

After Karl's family moved to the northwestern suburbs of Chicago, he and I attempted to stay in touch. But from the onset this ritual felt mechanical to me, woefully inadequate. Letters would arrive at my house with an odd postmark. He moved to a place where it snowed all of the time, and so his letters were filled with bragging pronouncements of snow accumulation, of school days missed. The Sears Tower was being constructed, and he wrote to boast. I was forced to reckon for the first time with handwriting as a substitute for hours of play we'd shared. My mom surely encouraged me to write back, though I recall few, if any, of my own letters. The process was nearly an affront to our friendship: our ease with each other was strained in letter writing and it became obvious—in the desperate, unacknowledged way that eight-year-olds suffer—that a once loyal and intimate friendship was quickly vanishing. We sent photos. The laxness of his public-school clothes was alien to me; he was metamorphosing into one of the guys we were warned away from by the nuns at Saint Andrew the Apostle, a pizza-faced half-grin in a *Cracked* magazine T-shirt. Physically he developed quicker than I; his fumbling attempts at growing a moustache began early, and his shoulders widened.

As a last-ditch attempt to remain in-synch with Karl I concocted a dumb invention: "the talk-a-letter." It had been my idea for each of us to tape record open-ended conversations onto cassettes, and then mail them to each other and record answers. Whether or not Karl agreed to this I can't recall. My memory involves a burst of enthusiasm for the project on my part, at any rate; I carefully recorded the tape, my anecdotes and questions. Before I dropped my tape in the mail I played it back, and the intimacy of my own voice embarrassed me. I knew that to hear Karl's voice after so many years would be a shock of a certain kind of recognition that I couldn't articulate to myself but was convinced would be uncomfortable. And, probably, unnecessary.

The vivid memory I have from this time is dropping my Certron 60-minute "talk-a-letter" cassette, bought for me by my dad at Dart Drug, into the bottom drawer of the desk in my bedroom. Karl and I stopped corresponding for good soon after.

Moving's a psychic experience, involving both spirit and mind. We remind ourselves of the elemental simplicity of this observation each time we startle ourselves inside of an empty house.

I grew up with the specter, not the body, of moving. My dad annually threatened to move us west to sunny California. The threats were idle, though warranted; the golden desire arose after a harsh winter in a house full of six children, and by the time Tax Day leveled dad, he was looking for targets. He loved the climate in California, and after returning from an IBM business trip would regale us at the dinner table with details of the sun, the lack of humidity, the gentle breezes. His Brooklyn-bred eyes would fairly tear up, but I sensed that a move wasn't imminent and was secretly grateful. After Karl moved away, my nearest close friend was Paul, but he lived miles away in Kemp Mill, too far to walk: the ease of strolling over to a home and yard in which to fancifully play was gone. But my trepidation at moving west had less to do with being wrenched from friendship's roots than with the fear of leaving the seasons behind, the narrative they unfolded each April, each October, each January.

So: fortunately for me, we never moved. Having lived at home throughout college I didn't leave until graduate school, at the age of twenty-two. Among the first friends I made in Ohio was a man named John, a biker from Pennsylvania with long fringes on his leather coat and longer hair who for the first few weeks of September slept on my couch and stacked his few belongings on the steps of my first-floor apartment. It was my first indication of the affective wear suffered by the relentlessly-moving. When I discovered that Amy had moved nearly thirty times in her life before meeting me, I silently vowed that I'd offer her equilibrium. An ingredient in her great character is the stoicism with which she endured her many moves; she had it all down to a rote, efficient display of economy bred with necessity. The thought of it amazed me. The prospect of moving west with my family always bothered me when I was younger, as I so richly and firmly related to the geography around me.

Part of that relationship left when Karl left, of course, as together we had built a dominion of imagination larger than any region. And my efforts to reconstruct our friendship frustrate me with their chronic lack of momentum. Memory's an illusion: we rub our eyes with glee, and the image disappears. There were few photographs taken of Karl and I together, for reasons I'm unaware. The images I do have of Karl revolve in a kind of kaleidoscope of desire and unease: I wonder how much of this meaningful time in my life I've developed through the erotics of my own memory, through the insatiable need for meaning. *Memory* comes from the Latin, where it meant, simply, "mindful." *Nostalgia* comes from the Greek, where it meant, abundantly, "a return." Implicit in the act of nostalgia is a yearning to go back, to construct or to reconstruct what is real out of what is desired. How often we call out longingly for the past through the cupped hands of nostalgia. The chunk of my life with Karl is tiny, but how such a tiny piece of time rules the landscape; how much of memory is there, and how much of memory do we want to be there. The dilemma will outlast us.

Time pulls. Through thinning fabric we make out the blur of faces, of body types, open mouths drawn into smiles or anguish, a canvas stretched tightly across boards. I study memories as a kind of art and engage them as emblems, representations, abstract or realistic, spare or painterly. Memories have stained the canvas, become an art-historical study. There's a reason why spectators are kept away from paintings in museums. *Don't touch! You'll soil the past with your oily fingers.*

Time pulls. We find ourselves ten, fifteen, twenty years later. Recently I was contacted by that vague yet ominously powerful force known as the Alumni Institution (wait until they get their hands on Global Positioning Systems, if they haven't already) announcing my grade school and high school reunions. The revisiting past took the form of daily generic e-mails and then slowly—one here, one there—classmates from my past began responding and copying messages on. Before long my inbox was filled with names from long ago. My first reaction was to dive in and catch up, my private nature charmed and stroked by the impersonality of electronic correspondence. *I can hang out in the corner again.*

In fact, I had recently been in touch with Jenny, on whom I had had a series of throat-tightening crushes as puberty had raged over me, Jenny whose hair swung in a manner bettered only by, no, not Farrah Fawcett, but Dorothy Hamill, the strong-legged skater whose white smile and thick thighs worked their way through my helpless sexual imagination. Jenny, who in fourth grade was part of an evil circle of girls who surrounded my desk and, making kissy noises with their pursed lips, chanted *Kisser lips! Kisser lips! Kisser lips!* at me until my red face exploded. (No. But I forever carry the burn mark.)

Jenny and I sent some light-hearted emails back and forth, and at one point I offered to send her a piece or two I'd written about the old years. She was living in Kansas now, married with many children, and I packed up a couple of essays and sent them off. Already I was feeling disenchanted with having reconnected with her. If, as Frank Lloyd Wright suggests, an idea is rescued and recovered by the imagination, then I found that I preferred the savior over the liberated. When Jenny's keystrokes steered her voice back into the present, the charm, the mystery—in a certain sense, the joy—of the past lifted a bit and she became another human in the world, not a figure in myth where I wanted her to reside. I have to ask: at what price should I—also a human in this world, whose hungers, stubbed 3 a.m. toes, and hangovers literal and figurative attest to the fact—insist on living with the myth and not the present? Can I continue to live like this, a pathetic dupe to the charms of the past.

Our newly-awakened correspondence was severed after the morning of September 11, 2001, as were so many conversations. Three months later, Jenny wrote to me again to confess that reading my essays had opened some old wounds, that she'd forgotten many of the details, thorny things at the time she was convinced she could not survive, and that, thankfully, she hadn't ended up the pregnant, wayward outcast that I'd remembered. It was all adolescent melodrama which she quite naturally out-

Looking For Karl

grew, though I insist on replaying it all as a kind of Ur-Recess Morality Play.

I had another chance to meet other mates from the past, and declined. My eighth-grade graduating class was meeting, and before long my inbox was again flooded with hyphen-altered names from the past, jockeying together in relative enthusiasms. Some people surfaced with a *hello-here-I-am-here's-my-life* email and then disappeared into the Web again for good, while others checked in daily with exuberant updates and tireless reunion arrangements. (I was amused, as no doubt were other of my former classmates, that the same go-getters in grade school were shouting out the old quiet types via email—as if the theory that life imitates the playground needed any more proof.)

Ultimately I was to be away in New York City during the reunion and subsequent suburban party, and Amy had little interest in attending anyway, so I resigned myself to remaining moored in the budding, acne past. Of course, later there came the photographs of the evenings, most of which when unattached from my emails I studied with some distance, unsurprised by the receding hairlines, thickening middles, general sagging of my classmates and their lives. What was far more interesting to me were the class photos which someone had miraculously unearthed and sent electronically to everyone. As in a dream the tiny faces of these kids again floated toward me, their grimaces of pleasure and suffering (the dreaded third-grade Photo Day, the fears of good hair/ bad hair) neatly but vividly filling in the spaces that so many years have opened up into a chasm of desire and longing. We were cute little guys and girls back then, and I was both pleased and humbled when I realized that a few decades from now the same kids whom I watch through my window

61

today trudging in the snow burdened by backpacks and woe will enter the same continuum that I did.

I was happy to get back in touch with a few people, namely Vanessa, a brash and curvy girl whose iconoclastic cockiness was the coolest thing that I can remember from Saint Andrew's. She was reckless and loud, funny and full of *joie de vivre* that was tempered by an hilarious cynicism coming from such an early teenager. She had moved to Germany during high school and fallen in with a Bauhaus art crowd, which didn't surprise me. On her subsequent visits back to America we'd occasionally head to downtown D.C. together or meet up at the neon-bar Poseurs in Georgetown, drunk on melon shooters and semi-startled, under the metronomic wash of New Order or Visage, to see each other again. I discovered that in the mid-eighties she'd moved back to Germany for good, where she still lives and works as an artist, and after we made contact again and I shared some of my fond memories of her, she wrote me back, pleased: "I'm moved your indelible memory of me is one of being an Atheist and not an Antichrist (as many remember me by)!" So, my imagination had redeemed her.

"Finish the story you started 20 years ago . . . " promises the advertisement on page 111 in the glossy magazine. "We'll find your friend and put you back in touch."

The search-organization calls itself *Old Friends Information Services*. An 800 number follows. Such a civil moniker for such a hungry service. I smile at the ad, for fate and circumstances have done most of the work for me. In a display of divine irony I've ended up living in a town less than an hour away from where Karl moved with his family three decades ago. That flat expanse of the country that loomed so exotically and distantly to me as a child, I now call home. Always in the back of my mind plays the loop of Karl, the incessant *ticking* of memory's projector. Though I don't particularly want to see him again, as the years have molded that fanciful world where he now resides, and I know that a reunion would be fruitless, I couldn't shake the presence of the old, old friendship. Finding myself in the local public library I picked up a phonebook for his area, unaware if he or if his family even stayed in the region for very long, and I looked up his family name. There were several listings of the surname, one with a "K." preceding it. For a few moments I envisioned tracking Karl down, visiting his home in the suburbs, perhaps stepping over children's toys in the front walk or entering a cramped, one-bedroom apartment.

    Like all desire revolving around my friend, this thought as soon vanished as it had caught fire, the traces disappearing into the air. No. I think I'd like to remain an eight-year old boy. Karl and I settled ourselves and our homes within the colossal nation of the imagination, and to meet up with him outside the border, passports in hand, would ignore what we had so carefully, and so lovingly, moved over, time and again, as memory's loyal citizens.

This Must Be Where My Obsession With Infinity Began

The Magicians

Rainwater pours into dusk, collects in gutter pools and in the brain pan of a mother gone gray with afternoon. Each corner comes on now. Sodden steps shake themselves free into foyers. A light's turned on.

At the Rec Center, the Magician shakes beads of rain from his coat, feigns majesty in the fluorescence of the large, blank room, unfolds weary instructions and presents himself to six or seven kids believing in the spirit of plastic cups and rice bowls and magic wands and cards before them, eager to learn the presences in the pull of dark corners and brightly dark sleep.

Later, they walk corridors to home, grim in the light fading fast. The Magician in his car sags out of the lot. He's going home too, they know. Props and gags rattle in a back seat, an hour over, strangers scattering.

Today the drive from school to the magic lesson a dull ache behind the eyes shut tight against the forest-green vinyl, the milky windows. Somewhere supper is imagined, and begun.

This Must Be Where My Obsession With Infinity Began

Margins of the Body

This Must Be Where My Obsession With Infinity Began

The Blur Family

The photograph is so grainy it looks like a sand painting. A family of ten circling platters and plates of food at a Thanksgiving table, sometime in the early 1970s. The scene's poorly lit, the shot is poorly composed—I'm imagining mom used a cheap plastic camera that she purchased at Peoples Drugs—yet the dissolving faces are beaming in the low resolution, warm, a snug circle. What's odd is the angle of the lens; it tilts the scene forward so that everything threatens to spill out of the frame—one tip from behind and the table will go tumbling. In the small room the family's crowded together at one end (*so I can fit all of you in!*) as if they're holding on underneath, steadying the table, the tall candlesticks, the dinner plates. The faces are barely faces at all. Not bathed by a flash, the countenances glow anyway, pillowy masks, dreamy abstractions hovering gently over varying body types, the details of noses, eyes, teeth, hair obscured. The more we rub our eyes to see, the less distinct the world is. Blurred faces around a Thanksgiving table: an archetype rendered beyond archetype into a kind of found art.

I know this family. For many years they lived in the

cul-de-sac behind us, in Wheaton, Maryland. When I was ten or eleven they moved to a new, larger home in a far-flung suburban town north of Wheaton. My parents would take me and my younger brother to parties there on St. Patrick's Day, where at night we'd swim in a heated outdoor pool. Moved away: we can do it physically, but the imagination calls us back to where we started. They'll always live in the cul-de-sac in Hippocampus, Everywhere, in an eternally messy house, nine kids banging around making noise and mayhem. The grainy photographs prove it.

Recently the small, face-shaped smudge in the bottom right corner of the photo made contact with me on Facebook. A friend request after more than thirty years. His profile picture was blank, or, more accurately, generic, that mysterious silhouette that brands Facebook members who've yet to upload profile photos, a string of faceless thousands looming on walls and in message threads. I checked: he still hasn't uploaded a profile pic. He remains an outline into which I can paint my many drafts of him. I spotted among his online friends his younger sister (she's the tiny blur in the top left of the Thanksgiving photo, sitting on her oldest blur's lap), and dashed off to her a quick message, sharing my memories of riding bikes with her and with Silhouette Brother, playing bocce ball in the yard, darting through the expansive woods behind their house. She wrote back. We friended each other. I accessed her photos, recent ones, and saw a woman in her mid-forties resembling vaguely the skinny colt who pranced in front of me down the trails, on the sidewalks. She's smiling a lot now, which is nice. She seems well-adjusted, surrounded by family and friends.

    The lens turned and focused. Her fuzzy outline at the

table sharpened into a real face, from abstract to representational. That I have difficulty matching up the two versions of my former neighbor—the girl then, the woman now—is, of course, my problem, and a precious one at that. Why do I prefer her in the photo of her blurred family? In many ways the image is a comforting placeholder, a moment in time secured in youthful anti-knowledge of the future's complexity, a family of young people I recall as still young, still laughing, still wandering eagerly around the annual block parties on their cul-de-sac, bikes and Big Wheels, fireflies and dusk. But there's more: I *love* the photo of the Blur family, the timeless happenstance of a cheap camera and low lighting, a smear of particulars that somehow cheers me. Their eyes are gone, dimmed to nothing, but that's not creepy; their smiles are sullied, darkened dots-per-inch, but that's not melancholy. What I love about the photograph is what trendy nostalgia-mill digital applications such as Hipstamatic and Instagram cash in on: a tumble into the comfort of a gauzy, sentimentalized past paradoxically made softer by a Polaroid's harshness, scratchy film that nonetheless soothes in its promises of eternal adolescence and a vanishing point that never arrives.

"Instead of just recording reality, photographs have become the norm for the way things appear to us, thereby changing the very idea of reality and of realism."

That's Sontag. I think about this a lot in relation to memory's slide shows. More accurately: nostalgia, that gateway drug to solipsism and sentimentality. There's nothing static about a memory, and yet I stop and stare. I pretend that a memory remains as still and compliant as a photo, but a memory is not a photograph: a memory morphs, slipping undetected

This Must Be Where My Obsession With Infinity Began

from one side of the brain to the other and back again, excising plot lines, adding characters, altering the personal politics of the figures. Though memories retell themselves at every opportunity, shape-shifters that can't be trusted, they do, after Sontag, become the norm for the way things appear. They do change the very idea of reality. What's real becomes *what-was* which becomes *what-is*. Try and frame that.

Looking at recent images of my neighbor, her face lifted out from another decade, now strikingly contemporary and detailed, brought something else into focus. One afternoon, decades ago, her older brother and I took her into the woods behind her house where her brother yanked down her shorts and scrawled a word on her buttocks with a black magic marker. She squirmed and resisted, and dashed off crying after he'd (we'd?) finished. A small childhood transgression that becomes eternal, its retelling shaming me with each half-remembered version, incriminating me in violence and bullying. I've thought about this incident often, naming the participants, implicating myself—but that was before I saw the girl, the woman, in her present life. Before, I had only the blur, the reassuring haze which erased her features, replaced her worrying cries with the whoops of play-dates, her urgent escape from the woods with cart wheels into suburbia. Now she's looking at me from last week, not last century. I don't know if she remembers, or what reality her memories may have altered. Her brother who friended me on Facebook—he was the one with the magic marker—is still little more than a generic silhouette. And I'm relieved. If he ever updates his profile pic, I may turn the other way, preferring the blur to the clarity.

Spying on the Petries

I shall therefore put my trust in the power of attraction of all the domains of intimacy. There does not exist a real intimacy that is repellent, Gaston Bachelard, *The Poetics of Space.*

I looked for you in my closet last night, Dorothy to Jeffrey, *Blue Velvet.*

A fable approaches me from a long-ago children's book, a slim paperback that's been drowned in the cool darkness of my parents' basement for decades. The book was a collection of Westernized "Oriental Wisdom," small parables and revealing tales spun through the ancient mouth of an Asian sage, brief lores buttressed by *faux* Eastern-style etchings of a black-gowned old man with long black shiny hair and whiskers, with venerable eyes to a Zen soul, pointy fingers clasped often in prudent reflection. He was a regional judge of some sort, and many frustrated townspeople would come with problems. The old man, judicious and fair, would listen patiently to each biased complaint and, simply but firmly, and always with an otherworldly detachment and gravity, dispatch his verdict, often a homily wrapped in a lesson wrapped in a penance. Real page turners, actually: I loved the judge's sense of impartiality, that no one in the small village was exempt from the law, which as he practiced it revolved around a broad and ceaseless value-system. I was receiving the same indoctrination from my Catholic education and home life, but perhaps it was my then-blossoming love for the romantic atmospheres of suburban Chinese restaurants that imbued these "Far Eastern lessons"—as equally aged, certainly, as Christ's pedagogy—with more integrity, more appeal. I loved the book, loved its ersatz spiriting of me to far-flung lands, and to wisdom, to certain primeval landscapes breezy with exotic lessons and timeless Universals. Reading in the air-conditioned balm of the basement, rescued by a house wired against the stultifying humidity of August, I felt as if this was instruction of a kind. (Of course, what did I know at the time of cultural stereotyping? That the book's imagery now feels to me flat and clichéd doesn't much register in the high country of memory.)

Next time I'm at this house I'll rummage for this book past old piano-lesson scores and collectible plastic NFL mini-helmets, perhaps retrieve it, hold it, but that's no longer the reliving of any past moment; I can no longer fathom the scholastic complexities of ancient wisdom then I can wedge my near six-foot frame underneath the pool table, where at ten I hid reading about Willie Mays and the Giants.

Why but for the passage of millions and millions of such minutes will I look at a retrieved book from my childhood thinking less of having gained than having lost. Over the years the specifics of these stories have generalized to a few emotionalized particulars, names changed, forgotten, etc. My favorite story from the dog-eared collection went something like this: one day a harried cafe/ restaurant owner approaches the judge and complains about a particular tenant living in the apartment directly above his eating establishment. The tenant is an indigent young man who can barely afford the place; the restaurant owner, out of benevolence and generosity, has no problem renting to such a risky prospect. All goes relatively well but for the day the restaurant owner discovers that the young man living above him, who is so penniless he can only afford a nightly plate of steamed rice for dinner, has been situating his meager repast close to his open apartment window so as to catch the aromas drifting upward from the restaurant kitchen. *Enhancing my meals*, the young man asserts innocently, exasperated when accused, *and in an honest manner!* The restaurant owner protests, *stealing smells for which you must pay me!* They end up at the feet of the judge, locked in incrimination. The young tenant is fearful he'll be forced to hand over his remaining life's savings to the greedy restaurant owner, who remains obstinate.

Having listened to both sides of the problem, the judge in characteristic fashion meditates on the situation. At length, he turns to the young tenant and requests that he remove all of the money from his shabby pockets—all of the money the tenant owns, as it turns out—and present it to the judge for inspection. The luckless young man fingers his life's last few pennies while the restaurant owner gloats. The judge asks the tenant to pour his few coins from one hand to the other and when he obliges, the clinking of coins is heard throughout the hushed chambers.

"There," replies the judge, turning to the restaurant owner. "You have been paid. This young tenant will pay you for the smell of your cooked food with the sound of his money."

This Must Be Where My Obsession With Infinity Began

Several years ago I had a strange if strangely satisfying dream. I'd been watching *The Dick Van Dyke Show* for the first time in years (the reruns had been a staple in my house when I was growing up) enjoying the physical comedy, the charm and decorum of the scripts, the roundly brassy, gratifying theme song, my obsession for place (*imagine a wild you don't know*) finding rich, fascinating terrain. I've always been intrigued by the Petries' house, by the ottoman, and by the movable screen between kitchen and dining room, the geometry of the living room softened by Laura's dinner parties.

And the adjacent bedroom. I grew up with *All in the Family* and I knew that TV couples slept together (Archie Bunker even wore the same style of pajamas that my dad did); the Petries' two single beds were odd to me, as to millions of other viewers. But the erotic potential of that bedroom: the episodes never filmed where Rob and Laura, drunk and giddy on gin and tonics and recklessly loud, push the beds together. Low lights and hushed cravings smothered, realized.

Suburban facade dissolving into a pool of hunger. Who didn't picture Mr. and Mrs. Brady "doing it?" Or when and if Mrs. Partridge ever "got any." Etc. But something in Rob and Laura's beauty and effortless partnership, in their Kennedys-in-New Rochelle demeanor and national dreamscape, registered in me as heartfelt, as something I wanted to believe existed somewhere.

where I crouch in Rob and Laura's bedroom closet. Botany 500 and Pucci, tweed and polished loafers. Theirs is a closet with Venetian slats. I'm peeping, staring directly at their bed. Rob and Laura Petrie are both nude, and Rob sports an impressive erection, over and down on which Laura slides her lipsticked mouth in a lewd oval, up and down, languorously. The dream lasts only seconds, splintering into pornographic closeups and back again to a wide, fragmented shots. The dream is in black and white and Rob and Laura seem very happy

My bizarre intimacy with Mr. and Mrs. Petrie certainly aroused me, but when I awoke the next morning what possessed me was the imagination's role, that somniferous vehicle lumbering down the poorly-lit alleys of my dreamscape. Why such voyeurism? And why the Petries? I didn't pretend to arch my eyebrows at some good REM sleep; the tactile possibilities of *Eros ennui* are among life's unbidden gifts. I was more bemused than concerned, curious than bothered. After all, Laura looks great in capri pants—erotic logic, unmoored by slumber, naturally probes. If indeed we imagine what we can't possess, what we desire, as that desire is our phantasm of need, what more understandably might the subconscious pursue then a fictional character engaging in a somehow taboo, unacknowledged behavior?

Fiction fans the flames of loss, real or imagined.

Many of my childhood memories originate near a radio. Few cultural signposts loom as headily for me as the odd Top-40 song with its attendant flood of faces, moods, anguishes, thrills. I actually believed that the radio was a tiny microcosm of a recording studio when I was young, that when I heard a song leak tinily from the transistor lying next to me at the local public pool I was hearing an actual simultaneous performance by the band *in the studio*; I never could quite figure out how the band could assemble their sound equipment, play and time their song perfectly in synch with the d.j., then, miraculously, do the exact same thing in an hour! And there were never any mistakes! It

This Must Be Where My Obsession With Infinity Began

seemed like very hard work to maintain a single in the Top 40, let alone the Top 5.

I had to imagine this, of course. No one indoctrinated me in this foolish belief, no older sibling passed it on to me as accepted knowledge for which I'd be ridiculed in front of friends. Rather, this was an affected curiosity, the reality that chose me, the fiction that was not. My imagination struggled to fit into a form it imposed on itself, in the intimacy of a kid making sense out of Three Dog Night on a July afternoon surrounded by strangers in bathing suits.

Now my aim is clear. I must show that the house is one of the greatest powers of integration for the thoughts, memories and dreams of mankind. The binding principle in this integration is the daydream. Past, present and future give the house different dynamisms, which often interfere, at times opposing, at others, stimulating one another, Bachelard

The house or houses in which one grows up fertilizes an imagination that blooms only when the house vanishes, imitation gold flecks of a picture frame scented by loss, reappearing when our backs are turned in the next state, haunted.

Apt then that our imagination will seek out intimacies in all form of house-shelter; Bachelard was sensitive enough to explore closets, cellars, drawers, shells, and corners, and later such abstract berth-contours as fire, water and, yes, dreams. A Barbie Dream House excites one's sheltering instinct as will a bird's nest, or an ant hill, a litter of kittens in a cardboard box—any asylum for the fantasy.

Fictional shelter intrigues us no less. My friend Jon, with his sister, used to daydream regularly and rapturously about

Spying On The Petries

visiting the Brady's house; "invited over for dinner" they'd spend an evening mounting stairs and peering around forbidden corners. I instantly understood and sympathized with my friend's desire, for we long to inhabit physically any space we inhabit emotionally. As a boy I meditated excruciatingly in an attempt to psychologically shrink myself down into my Hot Wheels race cars and to view my world from metal-and-paint. This fetish with fictional spaces can reach fascinating proportions: Beverly Hills postal worker Mark Bennett spent a considerable amount of his free time mapping, in architectural precision, room-by-room blueprints of fictitious television houses, including 148 Bonny Meadow Lane occupied by Rob and Laura Petrie. The sketches are collected in his wildly interesting and obsessive book *TV Sets: Fantasy Blueprints of Classic TV Homes* that includes, as well the Petries' and Brady's homes, fondly remembered interiors from *Leave it to Beaver, Green Acres, The Odd Couple, Laverne and Shirley*—even *The Jetsons*. Bennett's aim was to create a "utopian neighborhood," a domain of homes stylistically matched to your childhood reverie; to that end, his blueprints are legitimately buildable, workable, the erotics of desire actually put into practice. On pages 76 and 77 there's the Petrie floor plan in all its exactitude: finally, the identity of those mysterious rooms off the living room vanished down a hall; the precise dimension of the corner fireplace; the exact location of the garage; the bedroom. And that closet.

I wished myself into the Petrie's bedroom closet, trespassing onto their most intimate and private moments. The charge upon waking came not so much from stroked libido as from the oddly satisfying nourishment of the imagination that an artful transport into fiction can accomplish. Perhaps

This Must Be Where My Obsession With Infinity Began

I so longed to lurk behind the Petrie's closet door in order to create a physical space out of the mist of concoction, to make real that which I felt compelled to imagine. I dream fantasy into form, form into body.

Acting Lessons

Late at night in the deepening suburbs next to my brother I'd lie awake and peer into the infinite dark of the ceiling for my motivation: sleep.

Here's an old trick: in concentration lie next to someone whose repose is so deep as to mine the earthly turn itself, a soft, dreamed axis of slumber rhythmic in its deep breathing in, breathing out, and breathe along with him, each endless exhalation out, each breath in, and out again, learning the method of the body next to you until lost in the strange urge of another's dream you let go.

When lights come on, softly so as not to harm whatever image of rest the dark room developed—out of character reach for the other you've absorbed in the fitful night, learning to let go the cadence of another, to find whatever you've awakened as. Such exquisite, dark eyes you have, such dusky makeup you wear.

This Must Be Where My Obsession With Infinity Began

Bob's Blues

...their science clothes them like a garment, Roland Barthes

While living in the Washington, D.C. suburbs during high school and college I witnessed a rather infamous few blocks in the city's Northwest quadrant nearly vanish entirely. The adult bookstores and "arcades" (essentially video peep-shows: a quarter for a minute-or-two of hardcore fucking) leaned for years next to one of the few remaining adult movie theaters in town, which itself loomed over more adult bookstores and a gay restaurant-lounge known locally as "The Beef House"—next to another peep-show, etc. The strip ran along 9th Street roughly from F to between G and H Streets, a tiny area, but busy on weekend nights. In the early-eighties a large faction of D.C.'s pimps and prostitutes worked nearby and along Massachusetts Avenue before they were funneled away as so much livestock up to the 14th Street corridor. In the early- to mid-eighties, 9th Street, N.W. reeked of flesh consumption.

The area always enacted in me a struggle between heady thrill and nerves; being in high school and beginning to

This Must Be Where My Obsession With Infinity Began

venture downtown regularly from my protective suburban Maryland netting, the former sensation usually won out. I knew that I should be repulsed by such places, and on some level I was, but the physical knowledge that what lay behind those painted-over doors and inside those dimly-lit booths were films of naked men and women screwing, and not minding if I watch, indeed beckoning—well, the stock footage such voyeurism could add exponentially to my imagination's slide library proved too much to resist.

For a couple of summers I worked in office buildings only blocks away, but I can't say that I was a frequent visitor to such arcades. Fear and embarrassment would usually quell the empty (but roaring) lust, and I'd walk past. This lure, the pulling against attraction, was queasy. I envied those men who could skulk in at high noon and spend time indulging their libidinal urges—and at the same time their tendencies frightened and saddened me a little. The struggle between mind-knowledge and body-knowledge was a daily contest on this block. (John Donne made great sense to me while strolling down 9th Street, although I kept that satori hidden from my sixteenth century literature professor.)

The times I did tune down my self-consciousness and walk into an adult arcade, I invariably left poorer and despondent. It didn't take me long to realize that although the urges toward pornography were enormous, the satisfaction of those urges was sometimes less-than-satisfying. What was implicit in this struggle between the yearning for watching sex and the dissatisfaction with that behavior was the inescapable (if conveniently sidestepped) recognition that, while watching human beings fuck, I watch human beings. I discovered that the pitch to which my blood-lust sometimes rose while watching video of an anonymous woman give energetic head to an anonymous man was in direct opposition to the humanist respect I would offer any anonymous woman or man sitting next to me on the bus, or dealing with me in the office. The chasm between those two versions of *human* was enormous and always widening for me, then and now.

Many dancers feel that muscle contains, metaphorically, the ability to remember, to store memory. Might it also contain a will of its own, to deal the conscience (and the consciousness) selective, damaging blows? While I understood intellectually that pornography could be a dangerous and a damaging entity, I'm still waiting for my horny body to get the message.

We head to the Camelot strip club on M Street with the normal mingling of embarrassment and liveliness. Having sufficiently drunk enough beer to allow for *faux* shamelessness, we enter the club and are pointed toward seats at a rickety table equidistant from the stage and the back wall. The club is frighteningly, imposingly dark; it takes minutes to adjust to the low-level of predominantly red lighting. A woman stands on a small stage at the left side of the room; interestingly, what one notices first is not the woman herself but her images reflected in the misted mirrors, the icons, not the person. "Whoomp (There It Is!)" is blaring, soon after that ZZ Top. The woman is completely nude except for a waist chain and heels. She glows ruby. She may, at the moment we walk in, be clutching the center pole and leaning from it, or squatting at the edge of the stage encouraging the flow of money. We order overpriced, watered-down drinks and sit down, self-conscious. The woman dancing on the stage doesn't contrast in any appreciable way with any naked woman on any glossy

This Must Be Where My Obsession With Infinity Began

magazine page, or any actress in an adult film. The shock you might expect from walking into a room full of dozens of clothed men and a single unclothed woman doesn't fully register; the men in the room seem more corporeal than the woman. Our clothing doesn't so much heighten differences as it recognizes the imperfect material world from where we have arrived; the woman is so bathed in sympathetic, masking light that she appears synthetic. The effect is not of a naked woman writhing in front of men, but of men strolling past and gazing disinterestedly at an unclothed mannequin. *No fear of the human.* When you have drunk enough or at any rate feel brave or horny enough, you can approach the dancer with a handful of bills—your mating call, the scent of masculinity in the realm. You walk to the edge of the stage and if the dancer's eye has yet to be caught, stand awkwardly, waiting. Eventually she will slink over and gyrate for a few moments: the thicker your wad of bills, the longer the show. Depending on the establishment and the particular dancer, you deposit bills on the floor and watch the stripper dexterously pick them up as is her talent—or more conventionally, you slide the cash into her lewdly overstuffed G-string. Some men spray the stage with bills, and leave spent, while the grinning dancer rakes it in. All the while the music swirls and pumps, mating in blood lust sex and rock & roll.

Once in the National Gallery of Art's East Wing I became sparked while looking at a painting and instinctively raised my hands to gesticulate, to point something out to my girlfriend. Even though I stopped my arm halfway to the painting, the room's security guard was correctly on me; the result was a stern warning from security, and mild puzzlement from myself: *Why'd I do that? I know the rules. Don't go too near the paintings.*

But my body launched a *coup d'état*. When I was young, I always loved the children's room at the National Air and Space Museum; there you could touch genuine moon rocks, caress exotic foliage, let caterpillars and all sorts of long-legged, spindly creatures explore your neck, shoulders, arms. I still recall the aroused squeals of delight from all of the kids, the buzz in the room. That is certain knowledge, the mind and the body's mind wrestling for fun in the mud.

We discover at an early age that information received through the fingers and through the limbs—through the body—is as genuine and has as much integrity as that information accrued through verbal instruction, reading, or television. Witness the number of children's books that feature pop-ups or tactile, "touchy" gimmicks, the emotional value of hugs: as children, we want to be delighted from all angles, inside the body and out. During "reading hour" in my fourth-grade classroom at Saint Andrew the Apostle, Sister Nena would instruct us to lay our heads on the desk, and would then read to us a fairly lengthy story, patiently, languorously. The rich and deeply satisfying physicality of Sister Nena's voice, as it filled my sinuses and caressed my spine, always displaced the plot or the "meaning" of the tale, and indeed became the real attraction for me; I would be lulled to a point of near-coma, and lift my head at the conclusion greatly disoriented, melancholy. I recall several girl classmates whose reading voices had similar, tangible effects on me. Crushes all around.

The body learns at its own pace. Whether it's the ravaging, ultimate effects of regular drug use or the finality of carnage at the scene of an auto accident, the body's mind eventually comes to its own conclusion(s). There's no difference to my body between Sister Nena's tranquil, real physicality and a

This Must Be Where My Obsession With Infinity Began

porn actress' carnal, real physicality: the body simply responds. What was missing in my early, giddy experience of pornography, however, was the communion of the body with the mind. The marriage of lust and consequence. They'd yet to share notes.

As my fingers fumbled along the thigh of a stripper in front of me, a consequence of nerves and Wild Turkey, the shock of the physical was nearly too much. The tenor of the night certainly changed, and what protestations I had earlier mounted against leaving dissolved fairly quickly. The stripper's countenance, a fading mixture of boredom and fraud, instantaneously registered as my hand slipped upward along her leg. *This body is a person with memories, with photo books, a mother and a favorite TV show and* . . .

Sentimentally, I fleshed out this woman's complete life in an instant—no cliché too broad, no mawkish generalization too gullible. The moment was terribly real, and vaguely nauseous. One doesn't smell a human being from across the room, only when inches away; only then do the sharp contrasts in the room enter the body as blades. Unlike Damiel, the angelic protagonist of Wim Wenders' film *Wings of Desire*, my connection into the sensual world wasn't precipitated by desire for some breach of cleavage. I consciously chose the separation between dancer and myself; anyone entering a strip bar is forced to make that choice. In Wenders' film, the dented suit of armor that comes crashing from the heavens, securing Damiel interminably in earth's physical realm, acts as liberator. My physical glimpse was just as sudden, but rather than desired emancipation from flatness I felt an unwanted shackling to fullness.

Days after the incident, what I couldn't shake from my thoughts was the look on the stripper's face, its effect on me.

I ran through the usual angst-ridden ruminating: was it an inevitably dark, fleeting realization of my sister's sensuality? A cousin's? The devil's? Mary Magdalene's?

Bob is who most in our small town call "a character," and as is the case with many a man who has ingrained himself into the consciousness of a few, he dresses the part—in Bob's case, thrift-shop thriftiness. On our visit East, he and I sit in the Camelot strip club on a chilly November evening, neither of us having shaved for days—we're on vacation. The two of us look... well, dubious. Maybe even suspect? Not at all threatening, but peculiar. Men in dark, well-tailored suits crisper than their fifty-dollar bills sit next to us at their tables, looming like cologned sin.

We stare up at dancer after dancer. Bob, never one to luxuriate in material wealth, instead indulges a hopeless fondness for women, in particular large women—not in the popular New-Confession-Tabloid sense of the overweight, but large in an Eighteenth century rendering. *Zaftig, sumptuous, Rubens-esque, callipygian;* however delicately you wish to embody your desire into language, that very desire will clasp her ankles, bending languorously forward, and the delicately-handled words disappear with a cartoon-like "pop."

We stare up at dancer after dancer. We're poor today. Earlier in the afternoon we'd left the club with empty pockets and drunkenly blinked our way out into the commotion of Washington, D.C. at rush hour; grubby, we skulked into the subway and alighted near the Capital Hill townhouse where Bob was staying with his old friend. Our giggles toppled over one another like splintered glass into the settled, married tenor of this quiet house. We needed some more money but we felt as if elegance had been soiled by the stink-bomb. Moneyedup, we offered friendly goodbye's to Bob's hosts and tip-toed out of the house, vaguely guilty.

Back at the Camelot, we secure more-or-less the same vantage point and commence watching several more women slink up and back on the tiny stage. When the backing-music tracks pause in between songs the dancer looks awkward on the small, confined stage, sometimes frightened, as if a curtain has dropped between herself and the patrons and she's been caught, the fantasy punctured, nothing to do but stand there while most of the men stare down into drinks. When the woman stops dancing after her allotted fifteen-or-so minutes, she looks forlorn and slightly pathetic stepping back into her futile G-string, wriggling back into her tube top; it's back to waiting tables, and soon she'll be naked again in front of the same men for whom she's given drinks. As each dancer relieves the next, the women seem to share a common, gestural language, a secret.

If Bob notices any of this it doesn't register for here comes tonight's favorite, a woman with curved, prominent hips echoed in a robust roundness everywhere her body can echo; her personality, too, seems to arc in a friendly, cocky manner—to the degree one feels these dancers entertain with sincerity—and it's this pseudo-flirtatiousness that Bob responds to. Notoriously frugal, his self-imposed budget is soon tested in a playground-style melodrama: the dancer, entreating, sways over to Bob and myself and pouts, mimicking grave disappointment that Bob hasn't availed himself of her charms close-up, hasn't yet paid her for her service. She winks at Bob and flashes a wide smile, she come-hithers, Bob shakes his head *no—no money, no nerve—*; she frowns exaggeratedly, really working now, Bob, wanly smiling: *no—no money, no nerve, you're not supposed to enter me like this*—the dancer shrugs and dances off into the direction of two well-dressed dark men, one of whom has been sliding twenty-dollar bills into each dancer's garter belt with smooth, consistent efficiency all evening. Bob—bashful, tight-fisted—has no currency in this economy.

As we're leaving, Bob surprises me by walking straight toward the same dancer as she's standing in a corner talking with her co-workers. For a real moment I'm afraid that someone might misinterpret his drive. He stops short of the woman and says : "I'm sorry. I really don't have a lot of money." The dancer, amused at my friend's concerted sincerity and his discomfort, wraps both arms around Bob's neck, sings brassily, generously "That's alright, baby," and kisses him flush on the mouth.

Blocks away at the Metro Center subway station, drunk and fizzy, his masculinity restored, his club membership renewed, Bob walks around on his toes exclaiming, *I kissed a stripper!* as if our dancer friend was pulling the very strings herself.

"Striptease—" writes Barthes, "at least Parisian striptease—is based on a contradiction: Woman is desexualized at the very moment when she is striped naked. We may therefore say that we are dealing in a sense with a spectacle based on fear, or rather on the pretence of fear, as if eroticism here went no further than a sort of delicious terror, whose ritual signs have only to be announced to evoke at once the idea of sex and its conjuration."

But as the clothes come off a different cloak is draped. Witness the growing bulge of the stripper's G-string—nothing less than her money belt—as she pockets more and more control flowing from these men's wallets. The sign remains

This Must Be Where My Obsession With Infinity Began

the same for strippers of either gender, the body's topography cunningly similar in value: for a male stripper, a bulge signifies power, masculinity, control, dominion; for a female stripper, a bulge signifies power, control, dominion—and so, masculinity. That her bulge is heaped together by fisted bills of money implies more artificial empowerment than a well-endowed man's silhouette might (although he might be aided by an implant of another sort), and, after all, the female stripper's economy constructs itself through men. As a man pads a stripper's money belt he constructs her, the image of herself, her validity on the market, the essence of temptress, and vixen. She needs her customers, and they need her. The nightly evocation of Barthe's "terror" signs sure conjure the image of sex, but any pretense of sexuality is checked at the door of the club anyway, exchanged for fear. In their male customers these women renew themselves as increasingly-blurring cinematic memories, but as little more than that.

Bob's blues might reach him one day, Nena's stories will continue to ripple at the base of the spine, our bodies go on.

On Gazing

Boys freeze in the air as they leap from the jungle gym, hair lifting from their heads as if streaming underwater, mouths wide open, nearly hysterical on faces reddened by the long afternoon. And the girls. When I was a kid I dreamed of having the power to still the earth. It was because of the girls and their lengthening legs from skirts and their soft swinging hair that I lay in bed at night or cast my eyes head-down in church, and dreamed of stopping the earth's rotation. In the surreal stillness of a lifeless playground I approach any girl—in the feverish roar of hormones it's usually Jenny, Wendy, or Jackie—and she doesn't see, doesn't raise delicate and scented eyebrows, doesn't spin on her heel and rush toward girlfriends, leaving me in her wake of morning soap and confusion. I walk toward the perfume of her damp forehead, touch a shoulder soft and exotic under gradeschool white, run my thumb over a bra strap that from my normal vantage point might have been medicinal. To reach my hands toward nascent breasts and to lose myself in their give and take. To lift plaid skirts and to thrill at the rise of snowy thigh, the otherworldly cotton underwear, the startle of the other side of the moon.

Above me the sun shines forgivingly, behind me the nuns and teachers stand in rooms, frozen in poses of authority, looking the other way.

Sitting in a coffee house in town, my books and notebook open, what I want to do most is look up. And *at*. At a couple next to me, at a woman walking through the door, at an intense conversation among three people by the front bay window. Recently, a woman I know who's friendly with the owner walked up to me wide-eyed.
    "We just had Jessica Lange in here," she whispered.
    I knew that the actress was in town filming a movie for HBO. "Oh. When'd she leave?"
    "Just a second ago. She was standing right there—." She pointed to a pastry case no more than ten feet away from where we were sitting. "She had her hair pulled back. Had on a pink top?"
    I had been sitting at the coffee house for ten minutes already, and I'd missed her. *Oh, well*, I thought. But I spent the next few minutes reconstructing my entrance, recasting the scene in my mind, trying in vain to see a woman in a pink top among dozens of people already there. But I couldn't will her back: I'd missed her right there in front of me. I know what might happen: the memory of struggling to see her in my mind's eye will tattoo itself on me, and years later I'll remember *seeing Jessica Lange at the coffee house, right there, bent over elegantly, perusing macaroons.*
    Had I seen her, would I have stared? Respect for her privacy, and my own distaste for public fawning, would likely have prevailed, but the desire would be immense and powerful: to stare and stare at an ordinary, attractive woman cast by her skill and fancy into dozens of women artfully invoked.

Had I been allowed, by a god of stasis willing to freeze the moment, to simply stare.

I dream of living life in an erotics of observation. I don't want to merely watch, but to indulge myself libidinally—and, of course, to indulge who I'm watching. I want to luxuriate in the carnal act of close observation. Trees allow this of us, and ornate furniture, and paintings, and birds, before they skittishly fly off, aware of my staring presence humid on their envied plumage. A Canada lily allows me to approach it wantonly, to clutch surely but with reverence, to peel away scented folds, to plunge my nose deep into its neck, to inhale the life breath of the hidden world. But I'm not a plant, an unwilling subject might protest. Oh, but we're all plants, I cry. My writing students, plagued to inertia by the long darkening afternoon and the electric haze of fluorescence, come to life slowly, instinctively, when I raise the blinds and the remaining natural light streams in to bathe the room in a glow their blank faces lean into.

If my mouth parts slightly, if my lips moisten when I stare.

When I've visited New York City to live and work in the summers recently, I've been surrounded by subjects and objects worthy of close, erotic scrutiny. On a block on Fourth Street in the East Village I come across a building that stops me in my tracks. Researching a book, I'm on the prowl for the long-lost Wonderhorse Theater when I notice an odd bulge—there's no other word for it—on the facade of an abandoned building across the street. I am not an architectural *connoisseur*, so what strikes me isn't technical mastery of form and space as much as a kind of visible music, an other-century drifting melody with vague Mediterranean accents, a threnody for beauty boarded-up. I cross the street to get a better look, and find to my amazement that the bulge I notice is in fact a spiral staircase built onto the outside of the building starting a third of the way up from the street, covered entirely by columnar steel mesh. It's a kind of vaulted column housing steps, and it protrudes from the front of the building in a manner I can only describe as *nervy*. At the top of the column the year "1889" is etched in stone; from the bottom a long flag pole protrudes, drooping and nearly parallel with the grimy street. A pathetic and tattered blue curtain hangs from the pole, forlorn, half-wrapped around itself and tethered to the building in a hopeless gesture of gusty optimism. The building looks ancient, is anciently filthy.

My impulse happily granted me this June late morning is to simply stare. Hands on hips, I secure myself a good spot at the curb, crane my head upward, and watch and watch this building's decay of romance and fortitude. I'm obsessed with abandoned buildings, and search for them in any city or town that I visit. One of my favorite emptied buildings stood for years on the corner of 9th and F Streets in northwest Washington D.C.. Years before the city genetrified and spruced up the area, many boarded-up department stores and warehouses described the blocks, and Landsburgh's store stood immense at the corner, a giant weather pattern in decaying brick, countless windows shuttered with particle board. One or two windows remained unsealed, becoming errant homes for large black birds that drifted ominously in and out at dusk. Leaving work from a nearby office, or waiting across the street to see a band at the 9:30 Club, I'd stand on that corner and stare and stare at the abandonment, and the fulfillment, of space.

On Fourth Street, the spiral staircase doesn't really start

until the second floor: it hovers almost magically above a spindly, paint-faded pole that connects the column to the landing on the first floor. The building stands five stories tall, but the top floor seems to be cramped attic space with five small, arched windows, while the fourth floor gives way to an open deck in the center, flanked by two large windows, and the third and second floors look from my vantage point to be immense rooms—ballroom-size, maybe?—with enormous, arched French windows on the third floor and equally large, though less ornately designed, windows on the second floor. What I return to again and again in my staring indulgence is that vaulted column attached to the facade. What whimsical design impulse created this? It was certainly not a practical urge, as the steel mesh cage protecting the staircase allowed in the weather. If it was purely for aesthetic appeal, a vagary on an anonymous block, then I can say for certain that I've never seen another building like it. I lost the bulk of a morning standing and staring up at a building turned inside out to the elements, and to the watcher.

Once in Manhattan, walking, I followed a woman west along Ninth Street toward Greenwich Village. She was wearing a low-slung, sheer skirt, underneath which her black panties clung to and rode her buttocks high above long, pumping legs. I was hung-over, missing my wife, and had recently emerged from a porno video booth on the Bowery, desperately horny. I wanted to reach this woman and ask her to stop, *just so I can....* The same indulgence Amy allows me when she knows I'm watching her walk to the bathroom naked early in the morning, or when during sex I'm speechless behind her, the top of my head coming off at her submissive curves and undoing.

I didn't follow the girl far, a block or two maybe. *You know, women can so easily tell when a guy's looking*, an old girlfriend told me once. This I remember always and employ wisely. At the First Avenue and Fourteenth Street subway station a woman comes dashing into the car just as the doors are closing. It's raining, and the sudden storm has followed an oppressively hot and humid afternoon. She stands in the center of the car breathing hard, her thin dress-shirt soaked, her nipples brazenly defying her wish for modesty. I look away, but not before registering her damp chest and its rhythms, not before registering the look on her face of dismay.

Overheard:
"The absolute object slightly turned is a metaphor of the object," Wallace Stevens.

OK, but how will you know unless you circle the object you desire? If—

"*I have always loved backs,*" Phillip Lopate interrupts. "*To walk behind a pretty woman in a backless dress and savor how a good pair of shoulder blades, heightened by a shadow, has the same power to pierce the heart as chiseled cheekbones!... I wonder what it says about me that I worship a part of the body that signals a turning away.*"

In the far southeast corner of our large yard, in an untended spot, I'm drinking coffee, two cats at my feet. My gaze happens

On Gazing

to fall on two high weeds that, as an unnoticed breeze lifts, part from each other.

In a gorgeous moment, an ordinary weed pulls back from its mate, but two of its curled leaves are wrapped gingerly around the other's leaves. Softly, the breeze tugs at the weed until it's forced to let go, and falls—not far, a foot or so—away from the other in a momentary glimpse of complete, utter sadness. Absurd, what a staring body will bring to the natural world. I walk closer and am lucky that on this late-May morning the wind is barely moving, enough to enact this tiny drama in front of me. Looking closely, I see that it's only the smallest leaf on the one weed that is curled around an even smaller leaf—a sprout, really—on the other, but there is just enough membranous curl in both green hands to hook. A breeze lifts, and the womanly weed—she's tall, nearly my height, and verdant hangings from her strong stem suggest hair—is tugged back (by desire? regret? obligation? No—) until they part, and they both move forlornly in this transparent drama. Just as softly a breeze lifts and they join together again, leaves curling, stems urging along their lengths, and if I'm lucky—I've been staring at this for nearly half an hour—the breeze will indulge the weeds, and they'll move into each other wetly, rub along their stems and leaves until what's happening before me is nothing short of erotic. They might stop moving together for a moment, and a breeze will lift and begin the long tug toward separation again, two tiny leaves among dozens fastening to each other in green desire. An utterly ordinary moment made wild.

These are two stems from the same plant, and a ripening imagination blooms: brother and sister forced to part by Aeolus, their cruel foster parent. Or, lovers having to part. Or, a Union Pacific train roars by at the end of our yard and

99

there, there's the culprit! Two lovers at a train station at the ungodly moment of leaving.

The skeptic knows that the natural world doesn't tell stories, that what happens before me isn't narrative, but random chaos. In my sentimental indulgence I stage a theatrical erotics, the extras of the world cast together in plotted drama.

A man stares, aroused, at two weeds blowing in a breeze. Brazenly bored, two cats spread out among the bushes. He leans in to stare at two commonplace stems moving randomly under a high sun. He wants to reach out, but not to disturb, to caress, but not to interfere. The perspective widens. The large yard comes into view. An acre of jade, the trees dotting and shading, the circular drive. In the house the bed remains unmade this late morning, only one side disturbed.

I had a lot of creaturely fears growing up, one being that school friends were peeping into my bedroom window at night, those guys who bothered me in certain ways—like Andy, who'd stare at me all morning in homeroom, never taking his eyes from me because he knew that it tormented me beyond the edges of the history book I struggled to keep perched. This wasn't a fear of something actual, though, as much as imagined. I pictured Andy, Rob, Mike, etc., lifting a ladder up to my second-floor window and peering in and laughing and pointing at me during my private, after-dinner hours, when I'd close my door away from my parents and five siblings and indulge in homework curdled in fantasy: here my slack-jawed fantasies of prep-school sex with a bathrobe-clad Wendy fermented or, darkly, the irrational dread that my family was trying to kill me by poisoning the Crest tooth-

On Gazing

paste. In the midst of a fantasy or nightmare I'd whip my head around at my desk and try and peer through a dark window pane lit by the single desk lamp. The imagined presence of guys on the opposite side of the window—boys who I didn't know after three o'clock, whose homes might've been recklessly different from mine—was as prickly and lousy as if they had actually been there, lurking. I'd self-consciously stuff my Charles Atlas advertisement under my *1978 Washington Redskins Yearbook*, pretend to study, the back of my neck damp with fantastic fingerprints. At some point during middle grades I devised an imaginary, elaborate boxing-glove-on-a-spring that I could deploy from my desk drawer and that would promptly fly through the window and knock whoever was staring at me down to the ground and the indignity of Amherst Avenue.

Invisible on the subway. Invisible in the grocery store. Invisible at the mall. Invisible at church. Invisible at work. Invisible in the car. Stare. Vanish. Remain. Flee without fleeing. Love without loving.

    Gazing, I allow myself the dream I've long held: to become invisible. How I wanted to be able to float in and out of high school parties, a specter in an Ocean Pacific shirt, acne, and bad hair. One of the reasons that I identified with Elvis Costello's songs in high school was that his edgy, staring persona was often alone in a fuming corner, so ignored as to be transparent (*they say you're nothing but a party girl...maybe someday we can go hiding from this world*). I wasn't ignored at parties, I wasn't a social outcast, but I was never truly happy unless truly drunk, or otherwise lost with my eyes shut to the music—basic requirements now at the rare party that I'll attend. When Brendan came

This Must Be Where My Obsession With Infinity Began

skulking out of the bathroom, trailing a giggling girl, and came up to me and asked me to smell his fingers, I guffawed with the rest of the guys but really wanted to disappear, to float translucent above the party, not out of some other-century modesty or embarrassment, but as a way to get myself alone and to make some sense of the moment, all the while staring at hormonal confusion and ecstasy below me, kids scattering toward and away from each other to the sound of Depeche Mode and English Beat, lousy champagne, and the bewilderment of unclasped straps and unzipped jeans.

9th Street

Coming from the peep show I stare into displays of adult gifts and inflatable dolls, faces lined up row by row, rubber lips taut and gaping, sheathed like toys, astonished, holes for boring cocks. Alarmed countenances, some dismal song plagues the afternoon. They want their breath back so they can rise as the Trojan silhouette above them peels from the bath house wall, disused, fading.

Three arcades on the block lean against one another like winos, and across the street the theater is bolted. Above the marquee a figure, paint-faded, flickers into view, barely visible in a noon squint. I stop and watch long locks of hair stream acrid as light, a building rising as a face forever scarred white, dissolving among vestiges, a high sun.

This Must Be Where My Obsession With Infinity Began

.

.

Caught

A tame, mild afternoon. A high and welcome sun. Birds lift and dive in bright blurs around me. Near St. Mary's Cemetery my car idles at a red light. Bored by the radio, I turn to stare out the window. A flurry of movement in the car next to mine catches my eye: two college-age young women sit in the front seat, and I can tell by their convulsive shoulders and the music blaring from the stereo that they're having a good time. Nothing about their appearance is remarkable—they look like students I might've taught in class that morning. The girl in the passenger seat waves quickly for my attention and as I stare she holds something up to her window. It looks like a gift card? I'm betrayed into thinking that nothing's strange about this gesture, but as my eyes focus I stare at a photo of a naked, spread-eagled woman, forcing two fingers into herself in harsh, pornographic delight. The girls in the car shriek with laughter and bounce in their seats and the card winks in the sunlight. The cardholding girl turns back to me and fixes her face on mine, barely containing wicked delight; the mutually exclusive zones of our cars afford her boldness and she locks her eyes on mine and waits for my reaction with

This Must Be Where My Obsession With Infinity Began

the card pressed luridly up against the window. I look away for a moment in warm embarrassment and then, possessed by a kind of absurd machismo, look back, half-smile and give her an unsteady *OK* sign, as if to say, *Whatever. How do I respond to this? To vulva at high noon?* In a second the light will change and the girls will roar off—I'll hear their laughter over the engine and tires. Before I drive through the light I'll look around involuntarily, feeling as if I've been caught at something rank: there, a few feet away on the curb a young mother in cloddish pink-and-white striped shorts pushes her stroller in front of her, another young child trudging by her feet. Their backs are to me and their heads are downcast. They are walking in the general direction of the local public library, where a young boy can sit next to a young girl and, beneath the eyes of parents and friends and strangers log in to Yahoo or Google and stare at photos and read stories and letters more sexually explicit than anything I could have ever hoped to encounter at the same age. As I drive away I'll wonder on the girls in the car, on the young family walking the other way. What an absurd tableau.

Like all sinewy properties of memory, surging hormones are tied to a mess of images and stirring thoughts, a dank, dripping fistful. My carnal past: early, erotic longing for my sister blends with first, bewildering crushes and glimpses of panties on grade school classmates, learning masturbation after swimming in the neighbors' pool, coaxing my cold penis into the light of—well, something that certainly felt like wisdom in the shivering bathroom off the hall from my parents' bedroom. The quietly loud transformation of the *Washington Post* Sunday magazine ads: sudden erotic artifacts on the kitchen table next to the bacon and eggs and

Montgomery Donuts purchased after mass. As with any kind of body knowledge, nascent sexuality coursed through me with little regard to reason or rationality, as compelling a part of our physical relationship with the world as bone marrow, as fluttering, tired eyes at midnight, as hunger pangs at the end of a long, chilly afternoon playing in the woods. Do you remember the first time you felt hungry? The first time you felt lust?

Whatever shady memories I have of reckoning with sex, the one explicit feeling I can remember is fear—of the unknown, of getting caught, of not being able to look. For years the sexual urge for me nearly always began and finished in heart-pounding alarm. This had little to do with my Catholic upbringing, first at Saint Andrew the Apostle grade school and then at Our Lady of Good Counsel high school, because even as a young boy I understood the line between instinct and manners, and grew quickly to trust bodily yearning as a natural, not an evil or sinful, synonym for spiritual yearning. In heavy, musty art books, under the watchful eye of the mild, white-haired nun who tended the school library at Saint Andrew's, I first glanced at reproductions of Renaissance paintings depicting various Christian mysteries. Watching Christ writhe on the cross, arms and sinews straining, always spoke to me about the body's messy role in our future of agony. Maybe I stared fixedly, blanching at Titian's *Christ Crowned with Thorns*, studying the painful abnegation on Christ's face, the geometric glee with which His tormentors attacked His physique with civic policy: sitting in that small library room I knew that the body and that the body's desires (for pleasure, for surcease) were voices crying as surely to the heavens as any psychological supplications from the cross. And as a kid, I listened. I

This Must Be Where My Obsession With Infinity Began

was reflecting on the sex lives of our priests and nuns when my friends were reflecting on wheelies and The Fonz. After all, Sister Irene had legs, and knees, and the dark . . . Years later, when the rumor went around my high school that our school priest had confessed to a sympathetic student the Father's twin addictions to Pepsi and masturbation, it came as no shock to me. What was surprising was that we didn't hear about this kind of thing more often.

Perhaps the fear that I associated with sex had something to do with my parents. Not prudes, they nonetheless satisfactorily bore their obligation to create in their son a manifest respect for the sex act. Fine. Once, in the bright kitchen, I overheard my mother say to my younger brother Paul, in a dubious effort to sound hip and subvert his annoyingly adolescent brooding, "Of course sex is great, your father and I have it all the time!" I was less surprised than discomfited, wishing achingly that my parents would keep to themselves what they obviously enjoyed behind their bedroom door. Sex was not to be feared in my house, but the bringing of one's erotic desires out into the domestic realm was. When Paul announced that he was gay to our family not soon after my mother confided to him in the kitchen, what was hardest for my brothers and sister—and certainly for my parents—was not his homosexuality, per se, but his *human* sexuality. He demanded that we all turn to each other, recognizing, *Yes, we do all have sex lives.*

Getting caught, having the door thrown open onto your body's privacy—fear was bred there. I vividly recall the afternoon my father discovered the *Playboy* and *Penthouse* magazines under my bed. I was eleven or twelve, reckless in stashing the magazines on the floor knowing that my mother swept beneath my bed each Saturday morning. I was in the

Caught

basement when my father called me into my room. *Joe* . . . I remember large hands and clean fingernails. I stood with my head hanging as he towered over me, the vivid and fleshy evidence thankfully returned to the dark floor under my bed. Lemon Pledge hung in the expectant air. *I understand . . . a young boy . . . it's only natural . . . just try not to let your mother find it . . . it's offensive to her.*

My fear of getting caught (but why had I tossed the magazines so cavalierly?) was enhanced by the new, tactile fear of upsetting my mother. After my father lectured me, I fled the house in embarrassment and hurried alone out into the back yard and the warm May sunlight. Over my head I could hear the muffled roar of my mother's vacuum cleaner through an open window. Twin desires: flagrant lust over a splayed body, hurried hush before a buttoned guardian.

An event occurred around this time that stoked these considerable flames of fear. I had taken to wandering up to the local Wheaton Newsstand with my allowance on Saturday afternoons, but in the midst of the murkiness that was my blooming sexuality, an undertow began pulling my motives in another, pulsing direction. I was less interested now in the Topps baseball card-packs, Cherry Smash sodas, and *Mad* and *Cracked* magazines than in the rows of adult magazines that lined the top shelf around the perimeter of the store. *Club, Swank, Cheri, Oui*—the exotic one-word titles oozed a panting, Continental *joie de vivre* moistened all over by the cover models' lips and curves. That I had to crane my head upward to steal glances at these magazines suggested that my behavior was more properly suited to adults. And this merely basted the pleasure.

The Wheaton Newsstand was a narrow, astonishingly

This Must Be Where My Obsession With Infinity Began

cramped store; a visitor had to stand sideways to let another pass in the aisles, and customers were always elbowing each other as they read magazines. The air was thick with the odor of newspaper print, cheap cigars, WD40 oil, and air-freshener strips, and the owner, a stocky, florid man whose eyes I always felt on me, sat behind the counter on a high stool crammed into a space barely larger than himself. A general feel of fetid moldiness settled into the store many years before I arrived, intensified to my adolescent senses by the vintage of the sun-bleached magazines near the window and the stirrings of the ancient air condition unit humming distractedly near the back door. The clientele fascinated me: for every freckle-faced boy there my age, in would skulk a man wearing a long, dark coat, his head titled down, muttering crooked-smile requests to the store owner, which were incomprehensible to me but sounded alluring and vaguely threatening. A single shaft of light from the store's only window—a high, grimy pane at the front of the store—leaned a kind of agelessness in over us all and the ancient wood floor.

    I soon learned that the top shelf of magazines (they towered ten or fifteen feet above) were off limits to anyone my age, and it wasn't long before I realized that these were the very magazines, half-covered in brown paper, that were bought by the strange, slouching men in smoky coats and worn sneakers. I luridly felt and loved the pull of the danger in this place, aided by the owner's volatile temper, locally legendary, and that fact that, as I look back, it was the first place outside of my home that I ever ventured to on my own regularly. My body and my heart craved, and what those women offered on that illicit top shelf was too tantalizing to ignore. These magazines belonged to the world of *men*—large men with thick forearms and grunting manners, men like my neighbor four houses down

Caught

on Amherst Avenue who worked in the concrete pipe industry, whose basement den was done up in thick fire engine-red shag carpeting and wet, black leather chairs, whose cache of adult magazines my brother, his friend, and I had discovered in a corrugated box one day in the stuffy back room. A lifted cover: pale peach flesh and smiles urging a secret belonging only to men that we were too young to decipher, a magazine in carnal code. Men like my neighbor at the other end of the block, who for years would stroll past my house eating sunflower seeds, his bulk wasting away each season until he was barely there. I found out years later that the weight loss came from cancer, not exercise and sunflower seeds, and that every day he was walking up to his stool at Rosie's, the old-man bar at the end of the street, a hazy, grizzled memory.

One weekend afternoon I discovered that the manager of the newsstand had stocked a ground-level magazine rack with digest pornography, magazines like *Penthouse Forum* and *Family Letters*. My heart racing, I cased the store like a petty thief, strolling self-consciously up and down the aisles feigning interest in *Creem* magazine, soon recognizing that if I stood directly behind the rack, reached in surreptitiously through to the front, and discreetly pulled *Penthouse Forum* through the rack back toward me, I could prop it up harmlessly between *Reader's Digest* and the *Farmer's Almanac*. I worked up the nerve to try the plan one day and, hands trembling, somehow managed to squeeze a title through the rack and away from the prying eyes of the manager. There, frozen in the aisle, I could read about all of the lucky pizza delivery boys and horny cousins I wanted, and gaze bug-eyed at the crude photographs and back-page ads for "marital aids." For days my plan worked without a hitch; I was wallowing in the kind of stuff we all talked about at recess on the playground, material clearly out

This Must Be Where My Obsession With Infinity Began

of my reach. (See, right there: *For Adults Only*.) I can still vividly remember the oppressive, stale odors mingling with my roaring adolescent lust, fingers shaking as I turned pages secretively, as I peered through the rack every so often at the duped manager. I feared at every moment that I would get caught indulging in the body's off-limit world.

And so I remember vividly the instant when the manager's thick hand crashed through the magazine rack and clutched at the magazine I was holding. Startled, I looked up and saw his eyes peering at me through the magazines. The store spun away from me in a swirl of fear, and in a lightheaded haze I felt my feet lift from the ground. Memory seduces us with claims to legitimacy and to truth, though I remember graphically the long moment it took for the manager to sweep around the side of that rack and to lean down into my face, his eyes ferocious behind thick rim glasses.

Son of a bitch! He yanked the magazine from my hand and violently thrust it back into its place. His hot breath was on my face. *You son of a bitch! Don't you ever—I mean don't you never come back in my store, you son of a bitch god damned kid!*

His face was steaming. As soon as he began screaming, every customer in the tiny store startled and turned to stare at us. I backed away in fumbling embarrassment into a stack of wrapped magazines, shocked and bewildered that my action, however hidden, could provoke such terror. I fled the store and the manager chased after me. I remember his heavy boots on the floor behind me, my stomach climbing out of my throat. He leaned out of the store entrance yelling curses as I ran as fast as I could across the parking lot, and west along University Boulevard. I ran and ran and ran, my eyes burning, and felt that I was forever banished from confessing to public desire.

That incident so embarrassed me that it took me years before I could enter the store again, a sad fact because I had developed a true love affair with the place that predated any hormonal obsessions. When I finally visited the store again I was wiser, of course, and could thread the moment into perspective among other, larger rite-of-passage narratives. The manager, whose responsibility I understood but whose overwhelming invective I never could, was long gone. In fact the stand itself was soon to vanish, bought out by the Italian deli next door, to remain a relic in my memory, a pyre to lust and confusion. The intense experience drove me to satisfy in private whatever urges I had to read pornography, to never dare risk the fear of public censure again. And this slowly began to make sense to me: cloak an act so rich in mystery and wonder in wonder and mystery, respect the wild of the body with harness in hand. The moment at the newsstand stirred fear linked organically to sex, a breathless heart marathon that took years to finish.

"Check it out!" It's a year or so after the newsstand incident. My friend Paul and I walk through the woods behind Equitable Bank, two blocks from my house. It must be after school, as we're carrying backpacks. I don't know what we're talking about, idle adolescent chat. Rain has fallen recently and the woods are ripe with the mint odors of wet tree bark and soil.

Paul has stopped, now I stop, and we both look down. On a dark, wet tree trunk a magazine lies splayed open as if carelessly tossed there. On the page a naked woman is

This Must Be Where My Obsession With Infinity Began

leaning languorously along a covered bench, smiling. Dark brown hair falls behind her shoulders, and she squeezes large breasts between her upper arms, widening her nipples and offering her chest to the camera. Her hands and fingers stray downward, past her belly. She smiles. "God damn," Paul mutters.

It is difficult to sort memories, to sift through the past. What images lurk in us as emotional content obsess the dark, echoing garbled language. Perhaps our daily lives are nothing but a reckoning with our past, an image-by-image assembling of a haunted slide show. Is this all I have to show for my life, spidery pictures projected against a wall? There are no conjunctions in the past, no rhetoric to span picture to picture. A surreal panel painting. Blink and it's gone.

And so how to describe an image burned into memory, the lurch in the throat, the melt in the intestines when one suddenly encounters a naked woman in wet woods. The contrast between her pale, photographed skin and the black birch tree-trunk, the sogginess of the air around us, moist and fecund, the acrid aroma of loam and insect life in our noses and throats, and the woods—Hawthorne's secret, our secret, the high sun of another world of clothed mothers leaning in between gaps of the tree limbs above our heads.

"Jesus."

"Man, do you believe our luck?" Paul turns to me, his round face pale and dappled, a smile playing on his lips.

We crouch down together. The magazine is drenched with rainwater—it's obviously been here for several days—and the pages stick together like a rich desert. I try carefully to lift it but it is very heavy. Specks of dirt and soil pock the photo spread, the sun winks high above us. Paul and I grow uncomfortably silent, dispensing with our petty language now to speak a new silence with ourselves and with the naked woman. I stop to look closely. A tiny, pale-green slug drags a slimy trail across the woman's right breast, the world reaching up wet fingers.

"Man," Paul chuckles, standing up. I look and he turns his back to me, thrusting his hand down the front of his pants. He's clearly embarrassed, and now so am I. We both stand and reemerge into our world of friendship, slightly altered. I feel a great discomfort and resentment at having to share this moment with my friend, who feels now like a stranger. Our lean, overactive bodies speak an excited tongue we can't truly know and, standing awkwardly next to each other, we're left to navigate the gulf that emerged between us when we crouched over a naked woman, wet and giving of dirt.

"Yeah, I know," I mutter, forcing a laugh.

The magazine remained in the woods for weeks and every so often I cut through the path on the way home, alone, to look at the woman in the magazine. Each day she darkened a bit more with rain and decay, and the pages began imperceptibly to melt into the spring soil, returning as pulp and loam. Each day she vanished a bit more from my view, a siren in the dark, wet woods. A large gray snail crossed the photo one afternoon, rooting slowly. The next day the magazine was gone, taken by someone, leaving a trunk dark with wet, carved by a creature hole into which I wondered could I thrust my hand, could I stand the trembling, wondering what kind of loss my fist would return with.

Around this time, woods became for me a carnal place. Moist soil, the heady perfume of strong trees, long, cupped flowers filling with rainwater, bees eroticizing everything. To a boy

This Must Be Where My Obsession With Infinity Began

born and raised in suburbia, the natural world meant the odd regional park or group of trees unshorn by the newest apartment complex or strip mall. Across the street from my house stood Our Lady of Good Counsel high school, her athletic fields facing my street. Those fields sloped down to a medium-size hill that ended at the county strip and a chain link fence bordering Amherst Avenue. There were several small trees growing at the base of this hill and in the V-trunk of one of these trees I stashed a pornographic novel. Discovered luckily more or less around the same time that Paul and I found the magazine in the woods (some kid was dumping this stuff all around the neighborhood) the novel featured a generic softcore cover shot of a soft-focus blonde, and luridly hardcore fiction inside. I found that I enjoyed the kind of smut where I could supply the requisite imagery with my absurdly-hopping imagination. Never again trusting to bring such stuff into the house, I hid it across the street from my house for easy access. This book, too, suffered seasonal whims, and the act of reading the novel—fleshy with rain—became to me infinitely erotic. Removing the soaked book from the tree trunk itself was lurid, pornographic in its gesture, and replacing it each time snugly spoke to me of a bodily urge and satisfaction I was years from comprehending. Real girls were blurs on the periphery of my life. Reading the book with my kitchen window in view across Amherst Avenue, family members moving silently behind, offered a sickening thrill, a knowledge that what I was doing was morally wrong yet humanely right. I wondered in fear if my family ever saw me crouched behind the tree.

Eventually this book too disappeared, stolen doubtlessly by another boy and hidden in his secret place where he

Caught

too learned how the world will give up more mysteries and pleasures than he can fathom.

Washington D.C.'s old downtown used to be the place to go to find sin, before the area was considerably sanitized in the nineties. In great civic irony during the mid-eighties only a half dozen blocks east of the White House lay blocks of abandoned buildings, old-man bars like Ebbett's Grill, the red-light district, notorious gay and leather taverns, and the eastern- and southern-fringe of nationally infamous crack-addicted and bullet-riddled neighborhoods. The area always held for me a gritty charm—living as I did in suburban Maryland—and I would spend the humid hours of many summer afternoons prowling its blocks, peering into the darkness of boarded-up store fronts and indulging myself in the urban romance of faded bathhouse billboards and peeling paint, lost in the sun-faded ads on the side of ancient buildings, searching for Whitmanesque epiphanies amidst sleaze. At night, loitering on the corner of F and 9th Streets, waiting to go into a nearby bar or the 9:30 Club to see a band, my friends and I would laugh at the drunks and the shadows of men skulking in and out of the numerous adult book and video stores that then pockmarked the sagging neighborhood. These gloomy men reminded me of the men in the newsstand years before, and I sympathized with them as my friends and I would call out, "Hey Dad!" and look away guffawing. I had a glimmer of understanding of what it meant to be helpless in the face of lust; though I was usually able to pull its red fingers from around my neck, I often wondered about what it would be like to simply succumb. (Though a year or so later I was forced, embarrassingly, to beg from strangers for bus-fare money at the Silver Spring

Metro subway station after I'd spent my last quarter in a downtown porno video booth during my lunch hour).

At night porno arcades lit the street in tacky yellow neon and always held for me the lurid zest of menace and threat. Even later, when I was venturing into these places semi regularly, I always felt an outsider, a visitor to the den, my scared heart racing in that familiar way as I self-consciously read books and magazines or helplessly lost money to the X-rated video booths. It was on this block where Munther, a strapping Middle Eastern classmate from high school, claimed to have solicited a blow job from a prostitute. After she took his ten dollars her mammoth pimp materialized from around the corner, and Munther ran for his life. We laughed callously at Munther the next week in the cafeteria, and the incident cast the area for me with romance and intrigue.

One weekend in the dead of winter my friends and I decided to check out a porn theater in the neighborhood—that familiar, if vanished, passage. The Gayety Theater stood on 9th Street between F and E and was majestic in its dilapidated and crusty way. The building was very old, nearly wheezing, and in the unforgiving daylight its baroque architectural flourishes looked absurd and tawdry, especially in the service of promoting the X-rated movies screened there nightly. Much of the building now fades from my memory, the specifics too hazy to recall with much confidence, sadly. It was long ago demolished and replaced with upscale fashionable shopping; indeed, the entire neighborhood is unrecognizable to me now when I visit, the slatternly porno stores having long vanished, all of the empty buildings now occupied and thriving under the immense patriarchal shadow of the gleaming MCI Center.

Caught

In retrospect, we visited this theater during what must have been its last hurrah. Nervously gathered outside, drunk, and tense with the self-consciousness that plagues all young boys, we elected to send Fausto, the bravest of us (and, within weeks, a cocaine dealer) up the creaky steps to the ticket box. Moments later he came sauntering out the front door—I envied his courage and self-possession—and held up four fingers in the air. "Four bucks for a movie," he said, grinning.

"Alright guys. Wanna do it?"

Afraid, we shuffled in through the front door into darkness and mystery. The crisp winter air disappeared behind us as we walked into in a dry vacuum of stale, musty odors and the twin smells of bleach and disinfectant, sickeningly familiar from porn stores. To a high-school kid, it smelled of grim romance. Whatever grand "lobby" might have existed in the building's glory days was boarded over with particle board, I recall, and we were herded up a long, narrow red-carpeted staircase that creaked under heavy winter shoes and our loud, nervous laughter. At the top of the stairs, under a single red light bulb, a lonely man sat at a small ticket window, metal trim hopelessly faded, and barely looked at us under hooded eyes as we bought tickets. He muttered something to us in a voice that we could barely hear— it must have been about the theater's thin rules of etiquette, but we could already hear in excitement the muffled moans of the movie itself and were too distracted and restless to listen.

We turned right into the large, dark theater. When my eyes adjusted, I looked up and there, thirty-feet tall, a man was stonily humping a woman, his flabby ass wobbling as he serviced her, her wails and moans taxing the theater's cheap sound system. The sheer height and width of the screen and action was complemented by an extraordinarily loud

This Must Be Where My Obsession With Infinity Began

soundtrack, an invasion that nearly overwhelmed me in its luridness. This was one of the first times that I had ever watched fucking, and my jaw dropped at the larger-than-life action in this cheap theater that was spotted, it soon dawned on me, with a dozen or so men keeping rows of seats between themselves. I could barely make them out, but in their shape constancy their gloomy silhouettes of bored and hapless passion were all too familiar to me. I could see myself sitting here, hooded and alone, staring up and out into the privacies of gritty bodies. In that moment of turning from the lust and rancor of the screen to the hysterical solitude of the sparse crowd, I implicated myself. I've been tattooed.

We managed to tear our eyes from the screen long enough to find seats, a dubious proposition feeling, as we were, nearly drenched in sleaze. I remember that we sat together in a row, giggling like ten-year-olds, elbowing each other in wide-eyed embarrassment. On the screen now a long-haired brunette woman was lying alone in bed, her legs splayed open wide as she fingered herself into abandon. The bed sheets were gray in the chintzy grain of the print, and harsh light fell into the room as she played with herself in front of four teenage boys and a handful of anonymous men in the dark. "Pussy, cock, cunt," she whispered. "Pussy, cock, cunt." We squirmed in embarrassment. I noticed on the screen, near the edge of the frame, a phone resting off its hook on the mattress next to the woman. An amateur cut to a man listening on a phone in another, equally poorly-lit room, provided us with all of the dramatic narrative that we'd need. "Pussy, cock, cunt," she repeated aloud, over and over, scissoring in and out of herself with her fingers, rising slowly to a wail of—what, desperate, carnal want? It sure sounded desperate to us guffawing guys, who found the scene hopelessly hysterical and could barely smother our laughter, though this lay as much in our helpless hard-ons as in any kind of ironic detachment. The litany rose in volume and intensity, until within minutes she was screaming out the phrase at the top of her lungs, echoed in her body's tossing and flailing on the cheap bed. The deafening noise of the scene was absurd, and her wails echoed against the thin walls of the theater and loudly distorted the speakers, casting the scene and our experience with nothing short of surrealism. She shrieked over and over as she flagrantly spread herself in all her clinical glory. The phrase rang in my ears for days.

Around me, men sat as if dead. No one moved, no one spoke. They sat hunched down in their seats, their heads staring up from slumped shoulders in a repose of misery. A guy several rows in front and to the right of me was removing his hat every so often and placing it gently on his lap. Then, methodically, he'd lift the hat again slowly and place it back on his head. He wasn't bothering anyone, no one bothered anyone here, although occasionally a thin, wired man would turn and glare at us when we laughed or spoke too loudly; once he muttered something angrily that we couldn't hear. I soon figured out that the man obsessively removing his hat and placing it onto his lap was masturbating furiously—coming into his hat, was all I could guess. I found the camouflage nauseating. Around me, shuddering, I imagined that I could smell all of the sperm spilling around me, a tidal wave of jism fighting for life with the biting disinfectant. I settled further into my seat as in front of me on the large screen a woman was on her knees blowing a man while someone with a paunch was drilling her from behind, looking as bored and vacant as if he was pushing a lawn mower.

This Must Be Where My Obsession With Infinity Began

A couple of years later, in my girlfriend Janet's dorm room at 20th and F Streets in Washington D. C., a group of us—Janet and I, her roommate and a handful of people from the floor—stare uneasily at the television set. Hoodoo Gurus or Elvis Costello plays on a tape deck. A guy down the hall has a porno flick, and in fierce college-age progressiveness we all, at the cusp of adulthood, decide to watch for ironic kicks. The movie is called *Hard Rock*, and concerns a rock & roll group and their manager who is, or was, or might have been a groupie, but anyway who sleeps with all of the band members and the local dj's and promoters, and everyone else, too, all for the sake of helping the band get their big break. In the first scene the manager, a dark-haired, satisfyingly curvy woman, wakes her man up in bed with a blow job. Within minutes they're fucking furiously. In the dorm room, the mood moves from lighthearted to vaguely tense. We watch, feigning boredom, dutifully holding our girlfriends' hands or touching them chastely on their shoulders, and the girls squeal occasionally in dismay or disgust. Janet's roommate protests loudly but watches the movie through her fingers splayed open over her shamed eyes. The tape blares sex noises at us.

Soon, we decide that we've had enough. Midway through the next scene someone stands and turns the tape off, and for a moment we sit around in a stupid silence. My girlfriend and I watch each other warily, feeling as if we've stumbled into a script that we weren't prepared for. "I wanna watch *Rock Hard!*" a guy yells from the hall, and we all laugh with him, too loudly, grateful for the distraction. The party eventually resumes as someone puts on XTC or R.E.M. and we all start drinking and talking again. Through the night we'll steal glances down

Caught

at our bodies, hoping that we're still dressed. The girls will spend the rest of their night standing around with their arms over their chests in unconscious prudery, laughing softly, their faces made complicated, Bartles and James wine coolers, untouched, sweating on the floor beneath them.

I think of that small kid walking next to his mother on the sidewalk, by fate having looked the other way and missed the pornographic card held up for me at the red light. How surprised will he be when it does happen, after an adolescence of Howard Stern and Jerry Springer, the explicit, titillating commercials alone enough to induce hormonal spasms, or after a childhood of afternoons with advertisements of nearly nude, open-mouth girls spreading their legs in *Maxim* or *Details* magazines? Gone are the adult magazines covered over in brown paper wrapper, stuffed anonymously in long overcoats, carried like a kind of holy grail back to home or woods. In the adult sections of video stores, boxes advertising pornographic movies would with chaste stars block-out points of penetration on photos, but now the boxes advertise any and all explicit invasions of mouth, vagina, rectum. Soon will adult video-and-book stores bother to paint over their front windows? Or have they been rendered wholly irrelevant anyway by the Web? In public and university libraries, I'm no longer surprised to find computer terminals occupied by boys, high school-aged or younger, staring idly at high-resolution, color images of fisting, bestiality, orgies, semen-splattered faces of dazed young women—and often these boys are sitting next to young girls the same age as they are, or are slouching next to adults who uneasily glance the other way in vague support of the First Amendment. Under the grim reality of

This Must Be Where My Obsession With Infinity Began

fluorescent light, young people can see virtually anything they want now, anytime. The sad guy who I remember watching masturbate in a long-ago porn theater in Washington D.C. lives in my memory as an absurd figure of grace and comic decorum, affirming his urges in the dark in a kind of privacy. Gone is the search for the beast. The beast is out.

Nearly everywhere in the media pornography blares in softcore and hardcore permutations; it searches for us now, not the other way around. In my childhood and adolescence I had to harness my eros and urges, channeling sexual energy into the exhausting search itself. The fire baptisms I underwent were part of the lurid excitement; the furtive, guilty quest for pornography trembled in a kind of pure urgency and rightful anxiety. What I urged myself toward was a slippery slope into a maelstrom of noise and confusion and pleasure. In the swirl of lust, the three blurred so as to collapse into each other: noise, confusion, pleasure, one body! Adolescent races toward pornography were marked by a single challenge—finding the stuff—and I marvel at that which was fiercely guarded and censured now lounging around in the light of civic and capitalist day, not hidden in the dark, fecund drama of a shadowy woods or a tabernacle of tree-bark or resting on a high forbidden shelf as a prize awarded to the boy who dared the most to climb and get it.

When I was a freshman in high school, still dazed from the burden of junior high cliques and the excited bewilderment when gaping at Mary Rugerio's white hip-huggers, word spread around the halls and showers that Channel 50, a local television station with a notoriously weak signal, was broadcasting porn movies late at night. On Saturday nights after eleven o'clock I'd smuggle a small black and white TV set into my bedroom and spend an hour staring as a hopelessly scrambled signal twisted behind a flurry of poor-reception snow, all in the hope of seeing some sex. Occasionally, as if in a miracle, the scrambled signal would clear and on one-half of the small screen I might haltingly make out the grainy image of a woman reclining on a bed, beckoning to an off-screen lover, dark-gray nipples resting like saucers on her chest. Because of the scrambled reception I could never hope for audio, and soon enough the prone woman would twist away again in a transmitted shuffle, unseen civic guardians locking me in a snowy prison of adolescent frustration. Allegedly, my friend Paul received Channel 50 pretty clear in his neighborhood and, alone in my bedroom, walls flickering in gray silence, I made hot fists and cursed my sorry fate. How quaint the image of that kid looks to me now, fearing footsteps on the stairs in the hall, heart beating in hiding, craning his neck and squinting through tired eyes to try and make, out of a coarse and distant blur, a communion of private desire and a public, shuttered landscape.

That night in a dream I dashed from the pornography store because men with bayonets were charging the town.

This Must Be Where My Obsession With Infinity Began

Cathy or Katy

The rain fell through bus headlights, getting us ready for the big lie. We spent the weekend in New York City, my heart beating up through my neck in the gold glow and enormous doors of the Mayflower Hotel. Eric and I, when the urge to crawl out of myself toward her became no longer strange but strange and terrifying, left to cruise Manhattan, ending in a topless bar with hardcore sex moaning from each TV in the corners, where one of the dancers after having danced and swung her breasts before me gently and rhythmically, sat next to me and asked why I was in New York and (patting my thigh) honey would I like to buy her a drink? Eric (two months later he mounted an unconscious girl drunk on beer and gin in a motel room in Ocean City, Maryland because he didn't think anyone was watching) wouldn't move his gaze from the television, so I creaked something about a journalism convention. I said no. She glanced at the bartender who removed our watered-down, over-priced beer and asked for ID. We left.

Later that night I stared at Cathy or Katy and the thousands of freckles on her cheeks, the way her loose hair caught light from the desk lamp by the bed as if each strand were alight and moving, and imagined the soft dark inside her baggy sweatshirt and the way she would look through me and say my name or ask my name and realizing then that she had a brother and a father. She sat utterly unkempt, breaking my heart with every shift of her leg, or sip of her drink. Mike got a date with Cathy's or Katy's friend, whom everyone thought was prettiest. I don't remember the bus ride home, or much of the following weeks, when my fingers would tremble as I phoned her, and I'd ache in the surprise she expressed each time she knew it was me.

So I called less and less. I was relieved when I lost her number. I drove past what I thought was her house, and I wished I could be her brother, who endeared himself to her in so many domestic ways, his bedroom down the hall from hers, the way he answered the phone. What I recall: rain through bus headlights in the parking lot, with my house sitting down the hill. March. The rain fell as if on a great swell, and I looked, I thought, and saw ahead of me, over Cathy's or Katy's head of red hair, and saw little else.

The memory hole. Who, what, when, where, why, Cathy, or Katy. *A faint whiff of Catholic schoolgirl gleam-in-eye a peek down a white blouse a pale blue bra.* Did I meet her mother? Or was that someone else.

I caught fourteen sunfish on one bright, mythic afternoon. That I know.

I obsess on the motivation of my friend Eric who mounted an unconscious girl drunk on beer and gin in a motel room in Ocean City. A filthy beach house at three a.m., and I wonder if I really was there, in an adjacent bed, feigning sleep under pale blue sheets while on the floor beneath me, between the beds, Eric quietly laid on top of a girl and did what the hallways later said he did. Or did I hear the tale months later. Or imagine the whole thing.

I recall when my younger brother was born: a mother in a red pony-tail, a pale blue package, a tenuous smile in a garish photo. My parents said it never happened, I was never there. There. There's the photo to prove the memory correct, just as it happened, as I promised.

This Must Be Where My Obsession With Infinity Began

Length and Breadth

This Must Be Where My Obsession With Infinity Began

Colonizing the Past

When I was in college I pretended that I'd invented a small video camera that attached, virtually unseen, to a pair of glasses. I'd imagine wearing them all day, filming everything I saw. As in any creative sport, there were crucial breakdowns in plausibility along the way—where the film would spool, how my eyeball movement would be recorded, etc.—but I dutifully ignored them. Each second was captured, every class and walk across campus, the tolling bells of the chapel ushering in each new chapter. *Cinéma vérité*, starring: my consciousness. Co-starring: College Park, Maryland. I scorned Freitag's Triangle; the act of observing the world around me created the drama, and the struggle against dailiness provided the rising action. Conflict generated itself from the residue of ordinary acts: that girl dropping her books; that guy not holding the door for me; a melodramatic Hitchcockian Dutch Tilt at the woeful nickels and quarters in my hand as I computed the cost of the day's sole meal, a bagel (plain, nothing on it, thanks) and a Dr. Pepper.

I was diverting myself from student-commuter, bored, restless, twenty-somethingness. But as director of all

This Must Be Where My Obsession With Infinity Began

I perceived, I was also scouting my setting for content. Place as background, situation, mood. Place as metaphor — as what matters when I edit, when later I sift the subject through the setting and discover, hopefully, something meaningful.

In autobiographical nonfiction, place is elastic, no firmer than smoke. Nostalgia carries with it the desire to return, and memory its own mindfulness, less the urge to go back than the desire to stay put and try to understand. An autobiographical essayist's relationship to place has to do with his ever having left it. Memory erects a universe of civic construction, where things — fields, buildings, people — remain where you last left them. Physically return years later to the neighborhood in which you were raised and it can look like a cartoon image of overdevelopment, or decay. Changes look incremental to one who never left; to the one returning, the displacement can be overwhelming. But Nabokov insists: "One is always at home in one's past."

The friction between place-as-remembered and place-as-is warms any personal essay charged by its author with investigating the now mythic past. The danger comes when this warmth, sometimes startling, sometimes pleasant, morphs into sentimentality, a maudlin, grabby insistence that place matters simply because I once existed there and now I have lost it. When, in memory, I'm sitting on the low brick wall in front of an office building in Wheaton, Maryland, lovingly flipping through a newly-purchased three-pack set of Topps baseball cards, happy beneath the high Saturday sun, on my own and rich with my small weekly allowance, among stops at the newsstand and Barbarian Bookstore and Highs for a Slush Puppie, the impulse to sing it all produces

Colonizing the Past

a melody with both major and minor chords. ("No one cares for your tragedy until you can sing about it," says V.S. Naipaul.) Yet my loss is no greater than yours.

The past shapes and reshapes itself into vast proportions; the setting of my youth now glows as myth. The larger the imagined, geographic, and temporal distance, the more burnished and epochal that remembered place feels. Was. Is. This place is a lot smaller than I remember. It is huge.

When I was a kid I used to lose myself gazing at a particular photo of upstate New York, in the *World Book Encyclopedia*. I can easily recall the details: the hills' scarlet and gold, the toy houses, the quiet dirt road leading to a vanishing point. In the reading chair in our living room I'd spend hours with the picture, fantasizing living there. I wonder now if an aerial view of my hometown of Wheaton, Maryland would inspire the same wanderlust in another kid, if Wheaton Regional Park and the blacktop of Saint Andrew's might yet blur into legend. What I hope to fashion in any of my essays located back there is the recasting of an ordinary suburban childhood into the myth of same, stories that tell us how we came to be. Is it presumptuous of me to believe that my common childhood and its setting can be made into an apotheosis of kids and kin, pavement and place?

Google Maps allows me now to fly over my hometown, to revisit in three dimensions and atlas precision the places I've rebuilt (or halted the growth of) in my heady imagination. We don't yet know the effects of this on the cultural value of memory: the dream-engine that hovers over the past now competes with digital bits of verifiable information, cartographic certainties, calendar truths. I've spent hours on Facebook groups devoted to

This Must Be Where My Obsession With Infinity Began

my childhood neighborhood, where people I don't know upload photos of the very locations I've lovingly remade in my head, bonding us in an ersatz community of fond recollections and *OhmygodIrememberthat!s*. We live together now in a new suburban mall of remembering, collectively erected, simultaneously possessing and sharing the past. I'm not sure how I feel about these others, with their boxes of Polaroids and their scanners. They're moving in on my colonies of remembering, places over which I always thought I had sole ownership. How can my memories feel so crucial to me when everybody on "You Know You're From Wheaton, MD Because . . . " feels that way, too? The impulse to write autobiographically is born from this paradox, and the paradox born from place. Writing is selfish. Writing redeems that selfishness.

Stories

There are some that we come to in the silence of dust and dark, of living guessed at the fade of the corner, in the bleach of the particle board in a window frame in this abandoned building. 9th Street, 10th Street: I wonder at these evictions.

Behind my house there's a shack braced for the final fall, shut and open at the windows, limp from the wait: inside, a random moment remains—spilled shoes, a tilted book. A postcard pales on a table. There are words drifting into corners, familiar to the seasons.

This Must Be Where My Obsession With Infinity Began

Trains and Ties

Trains tell time. Dusk of a Midwestern mid-summer evening gives way slowly to a soft darkness: one by one the lights of a corn-fed landscape are extinguished, an owl hoots, black walnut and maple trees drop their limbs onto cooling grass, a quiet takes over. Our two cats sleep inside on wooden chairs that we drag over to our screen door, grudgingly curled away from a certain instinct the smoothness of descended evenings does nothing to temper. Crickets in muted rasps. The fireflies' brief flares. On nights like these, standing on my back porch, the only signs of the racing train at the end of our yard just beyond the back fence are the roar out of the blackness, the rattling of a door-jamb, the subtle tremor at my feet. Then a silence which drifts back over the yard, an exhaled breath.

During such moments—when, alerted to the approaching train by its miles-off whistle, our yard perks up an ear, and I find myself moving to the back porch—I am living in both DeKalb, Illinois and Coldwater, Ohio. That I can't see this train tonight makes no difference: this only solidifies the veiled clack-and-rumble into dreamscape, a certain kind of

This Must Be Where My Obsession With Infinity Began

faith. Such dreamscapes I've carried with me through many states and counties since those wilting August's in Coldwater. The rush and mystery of a journey standing awed and still, immobilized by the joy of an entire continent barreling by in an instant of fear.

My grandparents William and Frances Mueller lived for nearly forty years in a white, two-story farmhouse on South Second Street in Coldwater, Ohio, population 2,208. A second-generation German, Bill Mueller was a persevering, sedulous man who survived the odd tornado, the Great Depression (a generous boss at John Deere allowed my grandfather to take home money from the till, when necessary for groceries), and the bleak necessity of having to abandon plans for a formal education in order to tend to his family's financially-strapped farm. The third-oldest of thirteen children, my grandfather may have resented the inevitable familial responsibilities but this never showed; for years he carried around a thick, hard-bound tome titled the "High School Self-Taught" book. He learned about opera. He directed the church choir. He worked for 26 years at New Idea Farm Equipment as an assistant sales manager and, in 1964, after retirement, was elected mayor of Coldwater, a post he held for two terms. This I reveled in bragging pridefully to my grade school friends.

When I was a boy I anticipated August like no other time of the year, save for late December. Blissful, burnished, and bleached by two months of putting miles on my ten-speed, swimming at the public pool on endless afternoons, and shooting baskets until darkness fell, I took to the task of helping the family prepare for the annual visit to my mother's parents in Coldwater with relish (though it may be that my recollected eagerness has grown mythically over the years).

Trains and Ties

My brothers and sister and I would wash down the Ford Country Squire station wagon with buckets of sudsy water, attack its vinyl interior with 409 spray and the vacuum, load up on gum, Zotz candies, Tomy Pocket Games, and *Richie Rich* and *Archie* comics for the twelve-hour ride. We'd leave our home in Maryland in mid-morning, crunching up their gravel driveway well past dark—usually, as I remember it, my grandfather's silhouette rising from behind the curtain in the living room window as he left his beloved Cincinnati Reds' radio broadcast to greet us. Western Ohio on a sticky August night smelled nothing like the East coast; mingling with my sleepy disorientation was the aromatic proof that I was a long way from home. Cow dung, oiled farm-equipment, apple trees, fecund Midwest vegetation, the mustiness of Grandpa's cellar—it all conspired in my lungs to frighten my displaced soul into a kind of awakening, an annual foreign discovery so emotionally appealing to my nine-year-old sense of drama that I was relieved it only happened once a summer, so heady, overpowering, and instantaneous it all was. As my family stretched stiff legs and arms into the awkwardness of smothering kisses and *hellos* the lovely Ohio land began quietly to take me over.

In grandma's white porcelain and linoleum kitchen the window frames and dishes begin to rattle. No matter where we kids are we gather together and bolt through the kitchen and out the back door. We run straight through the backyard, past the apple tree, the picnic table, the well, making a clean breathless line toward the New Idea factory four or five hundred feet from the house. The monstrous back wall of the factory faces the yard, and in between runs a line of railroad tracks leading east into the heart of Central Ohio, west into the small center of Coldwater. The train whistle slices through the wind at our ears and we pull up at a small gravel embankment buttressing the tracks, and wait. My brother Jim is the bravest to peer down the tracks to signal the train's approach. As the *B & O* engine roars near and past us, my sister Jane's scream of delight—or anguish?— vanishes into the mammoth rumble of the train, now just feet away as it blurs past us, its flat cars and trailers loaded with farm machinery and cattle. The ground itself grips down, bracing under the rhythmic onslaught. I'm astonished that the tracks and ties don't rend themselves under the sheer continental weight of the train, screeching and shedding sparks behind it like devil's tender. The pounding in my tiny chest is overwhelming. My feet inch toward the tracks, an orgy of physics and myth. The last caboose flies by in quick surprise and, though my brothers John and Phil might have regained themselves enough to have motioned the caboose driver to send a departing whistle into the air, it takes me many minutes to recover from the storm and noise. Imperceptibly the bird cries and distant traffic on South Second and general silence restore themselves to the tableau. We turn and trudge toward the house. I am melancholy to a degree I can't understand and keep quiet about it. There are bikes to ride and parks to visit, anticlimaxes of all sounds and country colors.

When many years later Amy and I chose a house to rent in DeKalb, we did so partly out of fear of the train tracks running past the end of our considerable yard. Indeed, I was as concerned for the noise of the regularly rushing trains as I was for the traffic of cars and trucks out front, but I needn't have been: the yard is large and beautiful, our 1920's-era house is solid and quiet, we were sold. We took to structuring our afternoons around the train schedule: *here comes the 4:40; there was no 10:10 this morning.* It took us several nights to get used to the dozen or so trains that ran past between nightfall and sunrise; we've lived in this house for over a year, and now the night trains have taken their rightful place in our dreams. It wasn't until several days after moving in did we realize there are two sets of tracks; the first time we saw a pair of trains gliding by simultaneously in opposing directions we were astonished, like witnessing a magic trick. In the spring and summer we throw open our French doors open to the yard and invite the rumble in. It is as much a part of the soundtrack here as the crow and owl. I still run toward the train. Flat cars and trailers marked *Burlington Northern* and *Union Pacific*, loaded down with machinery and equipment, coal, hay, fresh produce, horse, cattle (and one summer, materializing in the bright sun, the lemon-colored, many-car-length train pulling the Olympic Torch on its way to Chicago) skirt past the edge of our yard and I marvel.

Recently a new family bought and moved into the house two down from us. Within weeks the husband and wife had transformed the previously spare backyard into an mini-amusement park for their small children. First a large swing-set and slide, then a volleyball net and all sorts of brightly-colored plastic yard toys, then finally an enormous above-ground pool, complete with deck. It's great for the kids: they're outside all day and into early evening, running and squealing, and I'm reminded of eternal afternoons, circa ages eight to twelve. Once when a train came thundering past our yard I happened to be outside and looked into my neighbors' yard in anticipation of the kids' delight. The

This Must Be Where My Obsession With Infinity Began

children didn't run toward the train, or point and scream, or even lift their heads out of the pool water. They continued splashing and dunking as the train bearing contents behind vented steel clacked past, finally pinching itself down to a dot on the horizon. Do we exaggerate the mythic dimensions of our childhoods, those prize moments that hardwire themselves into our memories and settle into our DNA? The fabled train, the lore of my past which ran through me as myth, brought forth no reaction from the children. Perhaps they've grown accustomed to the regular schedule of trains, perhaps they're turned off by the muted, industrial nature of the cars, or are warned against them by protective parents. Were two or three buffalo to wander silently down these tracks, now and again lowering their large heads and tufts of fur to the ground to eat, enacting the legend of the nation—would these children notice? Do I exaggerate the hauling through the human narrative that trains provide? Halfway up the yard from the neighbors' pool a sprinkler rhythmically patterns the yard. Their house is air-conditioned, sealed from the elements.

Once in Coldwater, near the town square, my brother grabbed my right ankle and wedged my foot in between the tracks that led behind our grandparents' house, with a slow train approaching. I recall scarlet panic and fluids draining from my body. I eventually wrenched my foot out of the track, limping away through laughter well before the train made its sluggish way through town . . . This, at least, is what I remember.

    I find it hard to believe now that my brother could have done such a thing, yet all these years later I've never asked him to corroborate. Was this silent-movie melodrama all a dream? Was I never the bound boy-in-distress but in a nightmare atop the large, vaulted bed in grandma's guest room? Maybe. Regardless of the truthfulness of this memory, the replaying (and retelling) of the incident has endowed it with verisimilitude, an emotional truth that stands for something larger, something actual, though I don't know what, exactly. I wonder how many trains I've actually witnessed in my lifetime—and how many did I dream, luxuriously? Before we lived together, Amy had rented a very small red-brick house in Athens, Ohio; whatever inconveniences the dwarfish dimensions of the house provided, the yard and vista behind the house were stupendous. Often we'd walk the half-acre or so in back toward an incredible sunset, an enormous sky canvassing Armargeddon's inferno. There was a train track that ran well beyond the yard, at the far crest of a small valley. Nearly a half-mile away, a long train crept by at toy-sized speed and stature, hugging a hill. The quiet filled our heads happily.

    This much I remember, and I know to remember. But the other trains in my life? Like summoning old lovers, I wonder if I've recreated some of the intensity. I'd skip my 19th Century English novel class in college to wander down abandoned tracks in northeast Washington, D.C.. Later, in Athens, I walked to campus each morning on old, disused tracks, barely visible for weeds and detritus, practicing each day to walk the rail further without falling off. When the rails and ties were later being dug up and paved into a parking lot, the ends of the track were wrenched up and left awry in the open field, the two parallel tongs pointing awkwardly up into the air, the end of the line indeed.

    It's part of the enchantment of trains that I can't disassociate their lumbering reality from their buffed, imagined lore.

And though I might question the odd detail in my memory of rushing with my siblings though my grandparents' yard to kneel in ecstasy at the thunderous train, the swell of my delight in remembering has an emotional vividness no camera could document. Time turns inside-out. As I write this a train once again moves with a dull rumble past the end of our yard.

In 1978 my grandparents sold their house on South Second Street and moved into a small one-bedroom apartment on the west side of Coldwater. My mother's brothers would drop in on occasion to check on them, to visit. As I recall it, the move from the early-century farmhouse to the modern garden-apartment complex, though sensible for two people each entering their eighth decade, dwarfed my grandparents, reduced them in a sense to mere dwellers. They no longer inhabited Americana—the house we remember and cherish with its sweeping staircase, hardwood floors, high ceilings, antique phones and fixtures, stuffy front porch where I sat for hours with *Reader's Digest*. They lived in contemporary America, became two very old people worrying about pills and falling down.

My grandmother died in 1980. My grandfather died six years later. By the time my mother, her siblings, and we many grandchildren gathered in Coldwater for what we thought would be the last time, the house had been inhabited by strangers for nearly a decade. We drove by, on the way to church, noticing the rope swing had long been removed from the apple tree. The well appeared missing from our vantage point on the tree-lined street. While my parents and aunt and uncles repaired to the church basement to discuss the practical matters of the situation—most notably the divvying up of my grandfather's things—my sister and brothers and I headed across the street to Betties Restaurant, a favorite haunt of ours when we were smaller. I vaguely recognized the waitresses (though the plump, friendly women might very well have been the daughters of the matrons I remember) and sitting around a black formica table we split pizzas and pitchers of beer, talking and remembering. The atmosphere was odd, as though it was somehow expected of us to recall our favorite stories and people. The hour felt somewhat stiff to me, predictable, which added to the melancholy of the long afternoon.

Hours later my parents and aunt and uncles came out of the basement, blinking into the sunlight. As she had looked at her father's funeral, my mother was drained though smiling, plucky and reasonably assuming that the others needed cheering up. As they walk across the street toward Betties Restaurant—they had arranged earlier to meet us there—I begin to dream: my Uncles Jim and Paul, soundlessly, their hands comfortable in their pockets, detour toward the center of town and, exchanging looks of blankness that hide a deeper resolve I can't fathom, stop at the tracks, bend down, and begin pulling them up, soft and malleable as flowers. As I watch from the diner window my uncles distribute pieces of rails and ties to my mother and to her sister. Somehow they fit into pockets. Somehow we'll take them home with us.

In the early 1990s, Amy and I drove from Athens across the width of Ohio to St. Mary's where we attended a family reunion. We'd arrived late; most of the food and drink were gone, and my remaining relations wore sleepy, late-afternoon aspects to well-fed faces. My secret agenda was to see Coldwater, though, and it wasn't going anywhere.

This Must Be Where My Obsession With Infinity Began

We decided, with two of my brothers and my sister, to drive the dozen or so miles south. It had been nearly a decade since I had last seen the small town, but so much registered so quickly. We drove past Betties—closed for the day—noticed with some surprise a strip club which wasn't in operation in '86, and drifted slowly down South Second to our grandparents' house. We parked across the street and stared for several moments at the facade, which hadn't changed much. John and Phil offered some anecdotes and blurred memories. After a while we walked toward town until we reached the old train tracks, then made a U-turn, and followed them back east toward my grandparents' house. We reached the back of the yard, and stopped. The air was still, the afternoon, though receding, was sticky and humid. The tracks were hopelessly weeded over, most of the stalks brushing my upper-leg. The day yawned. The New Idea Farm Equipment factory was empty, with the hulking, desperate stillness common to abandoned warehouses. Most of the tiny window panes were long since shattered, and a glimpse inside revealed inactivity.

We lingered there for a long time, remembering and smiling quietly, when we saw a group of three or four individuals approach us over the weedy field. Though they were strangers, their tone seemed friendly, unassuming; I thought they were the owners of the house, curious as to who we were who were standing around the desolate tracks. As they neared, my sister offered an exclamation of recognition; these weren't strangers, these were my cousins, Uncle Paul's kids. Slowly I recognized faces, body types, voices out of murky afternoons; we dissolved into warm small-talk. My cousins too, had felt compelled to visit the house, and the train tracks. They'd found themselves gravitating to an empty space which, bordered on each side by that which has long since disappeared, held at its center a hunger for return.

I knelt down and fingered the old rust on the track, flattened my palm out smooth on the metal. Listened to their voices, the long, dim cry, the final ride. What did it matter that we gathered here but that we understood time has no schedule. What was the real reason that we, a handful of blood, had arrived here? At a reunion people reunite, drift together, apart, or toward. As we stood together near the vanished tracks I wondered if this would be the last time. We were merely ghosting the present: it was later I realized that the last time had long since disappeared.

This Must Be Where My Obsession With Infinity Began

Suburban Abstract

A father throws his child up into the night sky: *dream hard.* A father throws his child up into the night sky: *when you wish upon a star.* A heat pump summons a child thrown: little ghost in headlights, little scream, little vision. A father throws his child up into the night sky—and what falls back? Dirt, pebbles, small change, deed, small tossed screams of a child. In the near future boys will spin aloft in the sky, fixing ways we breathe and think, new and improved constellations for each block. Look, look: *Boy-in-Air.*

If I wish hard enough, thinks father, my spinning son a stratosphere notion now, Sunday won't have happened. *Blessed notion. O-Boy-of-Boys.* He's on the dark side of world now, that dark dominion. Picture-window grace of composition, our little child tossed high above the pretty patterned yards. County checkers. At six, he lunged fistfuls of obsidian rock into the air, and once a hibachi ball, which came back, stunned his pals into agreeing *yes, this is stranger than this yard, this game*—made blood pour from the back of his head, a long tongue lapping at his blue T-shirt. He just fit into hole-in-fence, streaming home, rolling the red

151

This Must Be Where My Obsession With Infinity Began

carpet. You see, this child crossed boundaries. This child is thrown into the air, and his father thinks of history. Stay up there *to-be-named.*

Fragments of Terrain

I must walk toward Oregon, and not toward Europe. And that way the nation is moving, and I may say that mankind progress from east to west, Thoreau

I think of it as an early sexual experience. *Firehouse quantity.* My mom had purchased a utility-size package of matchbooks—there were at least two dozen matchbooks to a package—and she stored them in the cabinet above the kitchen sink. It didn't take long for an eight-year-old to sniff them out.

One afternoon, no one home, I snuck the package out to the back yard and settled myself on our brick patio. I opened the first book and struck a match, tingling in the erotics of sulfurous odor, the soft crack of ignition. I let the match burn down to my finger tips. That single match led to many others, and soon I was burning up whole books, two, three, four at a time. Before long, in a kind of discreet frenzy, I watched myself drop a burning match onto what remained of the package of matchbooks. I stared in awe and fear as the bundle went up, tiny explosions lacing themselves across an ordinary afternoon.

This Must Be Where My Obsession With Infinity Began

The conflagration eventually subsided, and I knew at once that I was in trouble. But my body had led the way: I couldn't have stopped myself had I wanted to. To my horror, the fire I had so blithely set had singed our patio bricks, leaving a black scar the size of a oversized dinner plate. I sat on my haunches and looked about, running a litany of defenses through my mind, surveying the damage. The plastic Mattel Cowboy and Indian action figures nearby, in the grass. They appeared to be fleeing the scene.

I grew up in the suburbs, which meant that I grew up with demarcations, with limitlessness.

I was always, and will forever be, a child of the Washington, D.C. suburbs. Land—neatly tended grass, the odd patch of fecund soil—was all around me, but I understood it only as parcel. I knew land as that which is owned, that which is fenced. Territories, our little yards; the dogs knew it best, sniffing the ground as if on the trace of something having vanished. I understood the world in grids.

My younger brother and I regularly visited an enormous hole in the earth. The hole proceeded a block of dense woods. The woods proceeded the maps. The hole was up the street from us. It's now full of cement and supports a bank and parking lot. Before the building came, people used the hole as a furtive dumping ground. Someone deposited a huge Styrofoam block that towered over our heads, and was as long and as wide as a dozen kids. My brother and I climbed up and jumped and jumped and somersaulted in the air under the blinding August sun. When we landed on the foam we disappeared into a splash of clay and dust. When I got home I was covered in dirt; it had seeped inside of me, was thundering along my blood. I was covered in earth, and I spoke a kind of earth tongue before I was hustled off into the shower. I had left behind a kind of jungle, a dirt zoo, and would never be the same again.

I climbed trees as if to leave the earth, because what we called the earth seemed too pleasant.

I love corners now, because I lived for too long amongst the ends of things: streets, limbs of branches, stairs, the yard. On my way to the pool I'd take my bike slowly on the path, the best to luxuriate in the coming bends and corners of the route (and, hopefully, to spy on couples kissing in the woods, all feral trees and moving limbs). I would stare into a curve in the path and wonder what lies beyond, though of course I knew. More path. But like the hallway leading from my bedroom to my parents' room at night: mystery is borne out of what we imagine we can get our hands around. The languorous, sexual bend in the path: a kind of flesh I lusted for. What would it contain? I love bends and curves for what they promise. The suburbs promised, too.

Tribal knowledge.

When my brothers and I walked past the post office building, there was always one door I dreaded. It was locked shut, and was never opened. It looked puny in the side of the enormous doorless and windowless facade. Behind, I guessed, were offices. My brothers convinced me that a man-eating lion lurked behind the door. This was our zoo. This was our African plain.

The neighbors' pool had a chemical leak. It seeped slowly beneath their wood fence and into our yard. White chalk spread itself into a widening moon-shape across the yard. It killed the grass. It nearly killed the dirt. It left only dirt. When I bent down to look at it, it smelled clean and fresh, like the future. Across the fence children splashed in the pool and played *tidal wave*.

I watched my best friend's gerbil when his family went on

vacation. It lived and ran fitfully in a transparent plexiglass cage, tinted yellow. One night it bit my forefinger through, nearly to the bone. I dripped blood so dark on the gerbil he thought night fell, and went to sleep. I ran my finger under the faucet in our bathroom, its perfumed walls papered in bright, tropical flowers. My blood spoke an exotic language I couldn't understand, though sometimes the throbs in my finger matched the pulse in my neck. I looked into the mirror and saw the whites of my eyes, and forgave the gerbil wildly.

The next day my brother and I played another game. We tossed a throw pillow from our recreation room couch to our dog, Molly. To our delight she danced with the pillow! First she grabbed it with her front legs, and then she held it close and shimmied and shook, dancing the tango with the pillow until she pushed the pillow through her hind legs. Often she kept dancing in a funny way after the pillow stopped dancing. The pillow was damp, as if sweating from the beat. Sometimes we put records on the phonograph and watched Molly dance her dog dance.

Bullies would chase us during recess at Saint Andrew's. If we slipped fleeing down a hill, they would catch us from behind and pile on top. One or two would open our shirts at the collars and stuff freshly-mowed grass inside. All afternoon during class we would stand oddly, and wear a language of green sweat. All Spring we walked carefully on the fields, looking over our shoulders in creaturely fear.

My mother tended a garden in the northwest corner of the yard, approximately 1/24th the size of the yard, precisely ten feet by three feet.

When we cleaned the gutters we dropped whole planets onto the driveway.

I left the suburbs of Washington, D.C. and moved

Fragments of Terrain

to southeast Ohio. There, the land bends over itself, its immodesty a celebration of fecundity. I didn't know what to do with so much earth. Dogs and cats walked in and out of restaurants. My head was drunk.

In southeast Ohio I had a favorite drive. I would leave Athens heading south on Route 33, past Shade, past Pratts Fork, and past Burlingham, pick up Route 681 at Darwin heading west, and take Route 50 at Albany back north into Athens.

For much of the hour-long drive I felt as if I was driving upside down.

Usually I'd slow the car at a certain intersection of two rural roads, stop, and turn off the engine. I'd sit with the window rolled down and listen to the silence, which said, *welcome to the other side of the glass.* I feared if I stayed still for too long, my car might take root.

Athens County sweats. One Spring, while reading Faulkner, I walked home and the odor of honeysuckle on First Street was too much to bear. I could swallow it. I thought of Caddy's muddy bottom, and Quentin's feral nature, and wanted to walk into a wall of dense green.

My house on First Street was built into the side of a hill. Once I entered after having been gone for weeks. I pushed open the door and walked into a cave. Vines and weeds crawling everywhere. I felt as if I could have pushed my hand through a wall of soil.

I slept that night and had greenhouse dreams: my bed dissolved into a pool of water and I could breath underwater. What was strange was that I could do that before I slept. It was a necessity in my new apartment of darkness and loam.

I made certain to pack a machete before I left.

The house next door to mine on First Street had a tree

growing through the wall. The girl who lived there showed me. When she stretched to touch the top of the branch near the ceiling her shirt lifted and I looked at her pale stomach, damp with fine sweat. I breathed in hungrily and wanted to take her upstairs.

They never got rid of the growing tree. It became a fixture in the living room, like a painting, or an end table. Those who lived in the house felt secure, as if they were being held onto.

The walls were often damp with sweat. Houses grow organically from the mouths of caves.

The dog who lived up the street from me—they called him Oven Mitt—one day darted through the open door of my apartment, headed straight into the bedroom, picked up in his sloppy jaw a stuffed tiger given to me by a girlfriend, and trotted out. Oven Mitt had never been in my apartment before. I never saw that stuffed tiger again.

After we moved to State Route 56, I took to standing on our deck and staring off into the woods. Once, there came a rustling from the woods so loud the cats and I thought a tree was splintering. Out dashed an enormous, dark buck, at least fourteen hands high, its antlers so tall and wide he bounded forward as if to catch up with them. His hooves pounded in my chest. In a moment he was past our house and at the road's shoulder, but he never hesitated, taking the two lanes in a single leap. He navigated through a neighbor's yard, careful not to knock over a single figurine.

The hills and ridges that surround Athens expand into a limitlessness that no map could deny. A kind of green ocean. Corners beckoned me with their usual musk.

A fence is shouted down, in the most charitable of ways.

The language I spoke with Athens betrayed a tongue that was deep down inside of me.

Fragments of Terrain

I left southeast Ohio and moved to northern Illinois. The language I spoke with Athens left me an unhappy, incoherent foreigner there. I was warned of the Midwest flatness, but wasn't prepared for this sweep of a land that seemed to have been tamed, shook out.

When I first arrived I took a drive, hoping some internal sense would guide me to a new intersection of stillness and crux. I chose a place; it didn't choose me. I sat near cornfields and a stop sign, and wondered aloud why no one was being nice to me.

I've found it very difficult to speak the language here. There are few nouns, and even fewer verbs. The dazzle of prepositions that cascaded over me in Ohio hang dried from leafless branches. The linearity of the suburbs expanded to grave sentences linked by semi-colon after semi-colon after semi-colon: a spare train track that clatters away.

The difference between the flatness here and the flatness of the suburbs is immense: what's multiplied here is not the land, but the lines. Not a horizon dotted by trees and phone lines, but a horizon overcome with sky. Because there are so few distractions on the land, one's eyes continually scan, eventually settling somewhere in the middle. A kind of surrender.

Driving long distances in northern Illinois requires a suspension of disbelief. One has to trust that one is actually moving. Corners do not lurk ahead of me here: all that can be known, is known. Is this a kind of wisdom?

My mother's garden was a rectangle. Here, I live in its neglected corner.

Disorder is clamorous, disturbing music, but it is music.

Once, driving up from central Illinois, we sped past a pig farm. Shocked by the bustle of scurrying animals we turned

This Must Be Where My Obsession With Infinity Began

around and parked across the road.

Nearing the fence, the mother pig tried her best to scare us away, but we were drawn to the dozens of piglets dashing in and out of every corner of the pen, maddening groups of bellies and tiny legs spinning in circles, lusting after movement. Beyond the straight fence which penned them was a straighter horizon, nonchalantly assuming the knowledge that powers it: order will not be swirled up into a frenzy of creaturely vigor here.

Trees stand on the odd horizon: old, old citizens.

Flatness as lore. Flatness as philosophy.

The train is a salvation: a line that moves lustily, and eventually leaves.

In the suburbs the frustrated homeowner builds with mesh wire a two-foot extension on the top of her fence, intent on keeping the dog inside. The dog will outleap the annexed boundary, and freeze in midair as I fall into sleep. Will I dream of what lives in me, or what's fallen away?

Forts

A snow-packed fort of dim tunnels and openings, intestines into the sides of the snow drift we dug. The patience of recess, the dig for lore a twelve-year old is surprised by. We dug, and dug, The Miracle of Antarctica at St. Andrew's, February breathing dark geography into our little half-lives. We dug, dug, dug until one of us became trapped, soft snow collapsing around the dream. The kid's name? Lost in the chalk. The cartography of this dark day: the bend of the gray of a tunnel corner, the quiet, quiet, quiet despair, a kid lost.

Somewhere it's May and a fort for the back yard is bought at a hardware store. Rough hands poring over virgin decrees: slot A into slot B, plastic bags filled with contents, finished by dusk. Boys sit in the cedar-chip fort with regulation window and nail-and-glue glumly reading of exotic tribes blinded by destiny, as the small, action-figure Cowboys and Indians in the Mattel Apache Fort lean in the air-conditioned hush of the dark basement, discarded, blue, gray, red, depending on politics, tool-and-dye, depending on history. This fort closed

This Must Be Where My Obsession With Infinity Began

with a snap-latch and was portable: the-past-in-motion from suburban house to yard and back again. Manufactured warriors, molded drama of paint and plastic.

A small boy peers into a fort pieced of twig and leaf, a continent of the day it takes the blackbird to move back and forth across the lawn. This fort leaves itself, turns, curls in the sorrow the boy might learn, later, reading some history book.

Transparencies

You approach an abandoned building the way you might approach a family huddled in prayer.
Remembering is the art of the cave dweller, Gerald Stern.
Prayer is a kind of remembering—that we are, that we aren't abandoned.
A deserted space reminds us that we have bodies, bodies which can leave us. We use the metaphor of abandoning where we've lived for many years.
Once I approached an abandoned trailer with caution: it looked like it could tip over. I managed to look inside carefully; there were enough soggy books and heavy boots to keep it righted.
You approach an abandoned building the way you might approach a family huddled over the dying.
Silence.
One abandoned building on a block of tended, well-fed houses. A kind of gravity.
A kind of gravity keeps me hovering near abandoned buildings. I'm pulled by the thought of memory.
The idea of the holy.

This Must Be Where My Obsession With Infinity Began

In some cities, abandoned buildings take up entire blocks. There must be a circus going on inside.

The phantom building.

Corpses are often discovered in abandoned buildings, especially in larger cities.

Who lived here? And what clues? The harder I stare at that corner, the sharper it recedes into the dark.

A lovely form takes shape in abandonment. Space renews its sense of decorum, its sense of grandeur.

An abandonment is like a routine hunger. Full, we move toward blankness again, on the search.

> In a field
> I am the absence
> of field.
> —Mark Strand

In an abandoned trailer a certain leanness. A sparse, hoarse insistence on the simple fact that we don't own the land.

In an abandoned house there's fragmented music that sometimes swells in early morning or the very late evening, when a breeze rises just so and a contentment fills the land.

A music you must stop listening for to hear.

An abandoned building is boarded up. A gag order.

Inside an abandoned building shadows gather themselves, their origins lost, their fluid dances stilled. They gather themselves and remind themselves that they are half-body.

What remains:

Ghosts.

A memoir of space.

There is no vision more haunted than that of the daylight

receding slowly in an abandoned house.
    A low cello note, held.
    An abandoned building reminds me: I have chores to do.
    I wonder often, when a church falls into disrepair, to what degree does spirituality abandon the space?

And what remains when disbelief has gone?
Grass, weedy pavement, brambles, buttress, sky,
A shape less recognizable each week.
A purpose more obscure.
    —Philip Larkin

    There is a purpose to abandoned buildings: they remind us to shudder, as if there were a spiritual life for us.
    And dust. And dry, cracked floorboards.
    We stop sending electrical current and water to an abandoned house. As if that will stop the life inside.
    Once, having broken into an abandoned building, my heart beat up through my neck and I looked up at stairs that never ended.
    A great, quiet calm can settle over an abandoned house.
    An empty house, an empty yard: we tend space the way we tend gardens, badly.
    The creation of memory: listening hard in the walls for stories, finding only the odd, lyric moment.
    When we infiltrate space with a building, we create a relationship between ourselves and the world. Abandoning that structure, we turn our backs on our loved ones.
    A deserted house fortifies itself against the elements, proving.
    A row of abandoned houses along a river. A row of abandoned trees along a river, *the bare, ruined choirs.*

This Must Be Where My Obsession With Infinity Began

You approach an abandoned building the way you might approach a family in the midst of a private mourning.

The quieter an abandoned house becomes, the louder the noises inside.

The abandoned farm house. The scarecrow.

A body hunched over, in prayer?

There was one abandoned house I could nearly see through. The next day, it was gone.

The Apple Carved

Martin Scorsese has consistently toyed with "the master image." The director, who carves out entire scenes of his films in advance on story-boards down to the closest close-up or the tiniest drop of blood, literally envisions his films, locating when successful the idea in the image. The master image is that frame that captures the "more pressure per square inch" that Ezra Pound attributes to great (poetic) art: in *Taxi Driver* the shot of Travis Bickle—alone, head down, hands in pockets—walking under the porno theater marquee, nearly overwhelmed by his own loneliness and the urban sleaze around him, was Scorsese's master image for the film. It ultimately became the poster for the movie in its initial release.

Having recently re-watched *The King of Comedy*, I pretend Scorsese's master image in that film to be the frightening tracking shot where we pull away from Rupert Pupkin's back as he stands in front of his imagined accolades and audience; it's delusional, the adoring crowd-shot reproduced on cardboard, Rupert adrift in his own vacuous, desperate imagination-cum-desire. As the camera slowly recoils from the scene we realize that we can't really be in Rupert's apartment: the walls are institutional in design, the space is far too large and industrially-lit. We're trapped with Rupert somewhere in the vacancy of his mind. It's a great image of the celebrity-obsessed, fractured pre-Millennium psyche, and it haunts.

If there was ever a master image for the sprawling, chaotic, flawed cinema-masterpiece called the Twentieth Century it might be Harold and Esther Edgerton's infamous stop-action photograph of the bullet tearing through the apple.
    Everything in the composition of this reality suggests the ecstasies and horrors of our age. The apple is perfect, unblemished, a freak of nature or a gift courtesy of touch-up photography; the stem protrudes toward us in cliché; the apple is located in space and locked down onto a metallic base; the bullet moves through the flesh with gorgeous, awe-inspiring absoluteness, its efficiency nearly erotic; the shot is composed with unerring accuracy, the stop-action freeze telling us that we've located reality's on-off switch, that we can now peer at and evaluate that which we could only hitherto imagine (quaint myths, Before Photography); the bullet drags our perspective toward the left frame with fierce but ballet-like dexterity, toward a future celebrated with might. The natural world is pinned down, found out, our machinations plowing through it like a freeway. There's some dignity in the Apple as Victim.
    This is an alternate Zapruder film: the genetically-perfected fruit, the blown innards soft and cottony. Violence staged, then perfected. Intrusion as Art.

I had both the fortune and the misfortune of growing up in the suburbs of Washington, D.C.. When I lived there in the

The Apple Carved

1980s the city reigned as the Murder Capital Of The Nation. It was national news (I think we'd dethroned Detroit) and it was kind of embarrassing, and scary: nearly everyday I drove down the same streets feared and lamented in editorials and news reports.

In a macabre burst of curiosity I found myself drawn to the notion of being surrounded by so much violence and death. I was venturing into the city from the suburbs to visit my girlfriend, who was attending George Washington University, or for afternoons in the museums and long nights in the bars, but I still felt nearly tattooed by the rising tide of violence in that city (an urban eruption nearly entirely in the Northeast and Southeast quadrants). What was shocking was the anonymity. Not only were there few faces on the evening news with which to sympathize, there were hardly any "people," period: I was amazed at the rising number of corpses, discovered by the metropolitan police in abandoned warehouses or apartment buildings, that couldn't be identified.

One summer I began a running body-count in the *Washington Post*. Each morning I looked in the paper for an account of last night's murders: I never doubted that there wouldn't be one. The fatalities rose exponentially with the humidity and by late-July the murder reports were pushed to the back of the Metro Section, especially if the discovered body or bodies couldn't be identified. A fifth of a column would be devoted to the news, maximum. Some mornings I read about as many as a dozen bodies which had been littered about the city overnight, victims of homicides. They were found in back seats of torched cars, in rodent-infested abandoned buildings, in needle-strewn parks, in dumpsters. I'd lost count by the time September, and college, arrived.

One morning, possessed by youthful righteousness, or

simply childish naïveté, my obsession with loud violence got the better of me: a news item reported that a young woman had been murdered by a male intruder. What was conspicuous about this account was that it printed the address of the building where the death occurred. I was used to a generic location, such as the "3000 block of so-and-so street." The specificity of the address tapped me on the shoulder; this death had a tactile quality to it, integrity as something real. I could locate it.

I drove to the building the next afternoon, either on my way in or out of the city, I can't remember. I vividly recall my heart beating up through my neck as I approached the particular block of Rhode Island Avenue. What was I afraid of? That the murderer still lurked? *Come on, Bonomo.* As far as I knew he hadn't been apprehended, but the possibility of a loose cannon felt quite remote. It didn't take me long to name that what I feared most was my unnatural, natural drift toward a kind of seamy documenting.

All a part of human nature, I told myself as I parked across the street. It had taken me a little while to locate the building; though the address was specific, the block of buildings was generic. Eventually I zoned in on a very narrow, pale-red brick apartment building squeezed between two larger, squatter buildings. There couldn't have been more than half-a-dozen rooms inside. I sat in my car and stared at that facade. What was I expecting? What, really, was I doing here? Pushing away explicit guesses of the murder's details, I imagined through which shadowy window of which room the murder could have been witnessed; I wondered on the time of death, and on what could have been happening in the adjacent rooms. . . . The building looked calm, unperturbed. And what was most melancholic to me was the fact that, indeed, nothing looked any different. Different than what? Than what I imagined it looked like before this one in three hundred murders occurred? The traffic streamed past me efficiently, in its purpose and sudden, high-minded resolve mocking my affected impulse to obtain humane knowledge about an anonymous event that I had no business lurking around. I suddenly felt sick, and started my car. I drove on, entering the traffic. I wouldn't be able to locate that building now if given a dozen chances.

My obsession for locating violence was really about my obsession for space, for geometric proof that the world exists in its niceties and its grimness. Gaston Bachelard, in *The Poetics of Space:*

> These virtues of shelter are so simple, so deeply rooted in our unconscious that they may be recaptured through mere mention, rather than through minute description. Here the nuance bespeaks the color. A poet's word, because it strikes true, moves the very depths of our being.

I can barely reproduce that building on Rhode Island Avenue in my memory, but it remains in me, emblematic. An emblem for what?

Scorsese, forced often to defend the presence and the explicitness of the violence in his films, shows us his hands: he's simply reacting to, and then documenting, the world. He once described an eerily daily event to *Rolling Stone*'s Anthony DeCurtis:

> I just took a cab on 57th Street, we're about to make a

turn on Eighth Avenue, and three Puerto Rican guys are beating each other up over the cab. Over it—from my side, onto the hood, onto the other side. Now, this is just normal—to the point where the cabbie and myself, not a word. We don't say anything. He just makes his right turn and we move on.

The violence in Washington D.C. had become for me so ordinary and routine that I'd wondered if placing myself in context would make any kind of difference. It didn't. We usually move on. But that building, that master image, represents a particular summer to me, one hot summer when I tried to locate myself in a space dulled by such rote violence that it barely existed. I rub my eyes.

There Was the Occasional Disruption

Weirdness lurked in corners of fenced yards and basements of split-level homes. Afternoons were orderly, of a piece, as we played aside the pleasant, luminous surfaces of homes and yards. Ugliness: acid creeping from a neighbor's pool into your yard; the stink of rotting food behind a restaurant; the sticky nests of spiders inside the abandoned milk case. ("Life is tough; thank God there's design," said Paola Antonelli.)

Randy was doughy, squat, with short legs. I liked his freckle-faced sister. She was soft-spoken, pale and narrow, with boyish hips and straight black hair that fell to her shoulders. They lived behind my house in the cul-de-sac on Bucknell Drive. The games would begin innocently. Kick the ball, chase the dog, climb the swing set.

In my memory, the gap between innocence and fury is erased, a Nixonian excision—such misbehavior was in the air, after all. Something gone for good. What remains is Randy's face, a comic balloon swelling, crimson with rage. Somehow, while playing with his sister and me, Randy became upset. The game stopped and Randy threw a fit, but

This Must Be Where My Obsession With Infinity Began

this was different from the tantrums we all threw, indulged in, sobbed ourselves out of. Randy, eight years old, looked murderous. His eyes bulged, his lips foamed, his small hands went stiff out in front of him, as if he was trying to strangle some invisible creature. He hopped from foot to foot, grunting toward us. His mom rushed from the house, scolding me, grabbing Randy by the wrist and dragging him back inside, feral on his leash. His sister darted away into the further reaches of the yard. Randy's home was alien; as far as I can remember, I never went inside. A glimpse of green ferns, velvety flocked wallpaper, a strange kitchen, a stone floor strewn with newspapers. He disappeared into the dark of the front hallway, screaming and thrashing. The next day I'd see him and he'd be fine: blonde and placid, stripe-shirted, grinning at me, eager for a play date.

After he erupted the first time, a certain minor note had been struck in the air, and a cheerful tone of eternal afternoons was forever changed. The glimpse I'd gotten into mania, the dreadful power that Randy couldn't control, felt like a peek into the distinct world of adults, of darkened foyers where dark, uncontainable things happened, where disorder prevailed behind closed doors. His mom's face was complicated, weary, and mournful. A year or so later Randy was shipped off to a "special school," the inside of which I begged myself not to imagine.

Walking home on Amherst Avenue, I looked up to see a boy leaning his head out of a window of the house two down from mine. A long, viscous rope of vomit fell from his mouth, a gray-white stream glinting in the sunlight, landing soundlessly in the grass near the air conditioner. One of the Emig boys. A muffled voice rose in anger from the rooms

There Was the Occasional Disruption

behind him; I matched it to a vague, motherly face. I was too young to know anything about hidden drinking or hangovers, but the lurid wrongness of it all stained the afternoon. Something in the headlong rush of it, the soft head bobbing forlornly out of the window, the alarm sounding behind him in the split-level house said *shame,* before I knew the word. I don't know: maybe he had a stomach virus, or food poisoning. But why retch out the bedroom window, turning a private moment public? I knew without knowing that the Emig boy was holed up in his bedroom in misery, trying to hide.

What begins as rumor can never circle back to fact, instead moves inevitably toward myth. She was elderly and lived a half mile away on Arcola Avenue, in a home set back from the street. There was a large plate-glass window in front: one day someone fired a bullet through the window that killed her. This is a fact, yet the news arrived to me less as information than as a gloomy song, a melody that lingered from earlier eras. That is: I don't remember the incident, I remember the telling and the re-telling. I know little about her except what I've imagined, and what I've imagined is awful. How do I posses an image of a white head of hair, of a small woman sitting at her kitchen table in front of a window, mildly staring into the middle distance? Around this time two young girls, the Lyon sisters, vanished from Wheaton Plaza near my house. For years their gradeschool photos, affecting and tragic in black and white, hung in post offices and stores, casting-call sheets for our communal and ongoing nightmares of *What Happened* and *What If.* I had— I have—the grainy photos as evidence that these young girls existed. Four decades later, they're still gone. For a year after

This Must Be Where My Obsession With Infinity Began

the Arcola Avenue shooting—which was random, and also, as far as I know, an unsolved mystery—I'd walk or bike past her house on my way home from Saint Andrew's, and her front window became a kind of screen onto which I'd project stories of what had happened, and why, silhouetted hoods, glass shattering impossibly, of family members I never knew but imagined in their noiseless grief, but I'd always circle back to a woman, sitting, her hands clasped gently on the top of the table, the details of the kitchen behind her blurring.

Our family's spending a week at Rehoboth Beach in Delaware, where we've rented a house. I'm lying in bed in the room I share with my younger brother, trying to doze, broiling with sunburn in the air conditioning, listening through the thin walls to my older brothers in the next room. One of them is telling a story of which I can make out muffled parts. A boy they knew from high school walked to the train tracks and laid down on them. *No I don't want to hear this—but I'm going to tell you—*. The train barreled down the tracks and screamed its whistle and . . . . *I don't wanna hear this—*. One of my brothers whimpers, or cries out. My brother telling the story is insistent, he will finish. The night's fabric is torn, and I deeply regret my childish urge to eavesdrop. I stay awake for most of the night, upset with my brothers for talking in the dark. Braced for ugliness and disorder I still couldn't name, I brought this story back to the suburbs, a new, eccentric thumping in my chest.

Student Killed by Freight Train

I think somehow that I can fill space, once bereaved, with living space, with space that warms. I stand from a log on the gravel lot behind the Lincoln Inn Restaurant and walk the five or so feet back to the train tracks where a long Union Pacific freight train has just finished rumbling past, groaning ties beneath it, shedding sparks and cries. As it disappears out of town to the east, I step closer, my ears humming in the new calm, lean down to place my palm on the rail. The steel is cold. Strange. Out of the corner of my eye I notice a man twenty or so feet down the track. He's standing from having touched the rail with his hand, too.

"Weird," I call out to him. I'm befuddled. "I thought it'd be hot. Nothing."

"Yeah," he calls back with a half-grin. "Not a thing."

He shrugs his shoulders and walks back to his car. I stare back down at the rail, confused, expectant. The sun is high and bright, odd for mid-November. Were I to later bring a tuning fork to the rail and strike, I might hear in the resonance a single, held note pealed from the beauty and the trouble of locomotion.

This Must Be Where My Obsession With Infinity Began

3:45 a.m.. The young man looks with dark eyes into a lobby grimly lit by the fluorescence of civic hospitality, a *Welcome* mat eked out in chains across the Midwest. Not a soul for hours. He had told his friends. And he had told her. In the garish lighting of the Best Western Inn and Suites on West Lincoln Highway he sat behind the paneled front desk, leaning his tired head out over his body, the tingling of sadness having long vanished. He couldn't tell what had replaced it. He had told his friends. He called the last friend a little over an hour ago. *I wonder what. How they'll deal.* It's a short walk from the lobby, through the front glass doors, past the east wing of rooms, past the warm, homey scent of the laundry room, past the twin dumpsters, past the few parked cars and semi's, toward the edge of the parking lot, into the grass now dark and discreet with sleep, over the crunchy thistle and gravel, over the chain link fence, just ten or so feet now up a small embankment to the tracks. The night is still and, actually, the night is impossibly gorgeous. It's probably four in the morning. *Wonder what.* The track is not as cold as he thought. The ties are uncomfortable, much wider apart than he would've thought. He felt the rumble a minute or so before the whistle *funny like Radar M*A*S*H* his dog Jasmine the faded linoleum remember when you held the neighbor's puppy on your stomach in the middle of the kitchen floor and you knew that you made such a cute picture that you'd wait until someone came in but no one came in and looked so you felt stupid and you pretended to be asleep in the middle of the kitchen floor? the rumble is so loud now he feels it in his sinuses and down the canal of his spine God this hurts a long thin space filling with sound and vibration and he feels that the dark and spacious sky is pulsing in a minor key now it feels like he'll be pushed off the track by the speed and shaking *wonder how* the whistle is piercingly loud God how do people live here? how do people? the terrible screech of brakes a loud manly or unearthly scream but no it can't be the conductor's and no it can't be his and he had told people the dark

It's one of my favorite sounds: the long cry of a train whistle. A Baltimore & Ohio track ran the length of my grandparents' yard in Coldwater, Ohio and as a kid I loved running out to the tracks after I'd heard the faint whistle come from over the corn fields and neighboring farms—my body hearing first, an animal to an inaudible cry. The train might as well have been coming across an infinity of land, from the wavy mirage that was Indiana. The sinewy, impossible grace of those tracks, their masculine arch over the country, the solitude and sadness of the moments after the train had roared by, the dream over, the transcendence settling, myself made visible again. All of this conspired with a long-ago image of brown, sad buffalo chewing up long, pale-green grass that had grown between the ties in an abandoned rail yard. Where'd I see that picture? In a school book, or an afternoon movie? Wherever I happen to live I look for trains, listen for trains, stay up in bed during wakeful nights lamenting that I wasn't raised near them, prizing the lives of those boys who grew up along them, who knew the thunder, felt it fill in the heavy spaces in their bodies. As a boy in suburban environs, I envied those boys as I envied those who grew up along rivers, those winding, dark pretenders to the nobility and mystery of the trains.

I listened hard to the air the day after a twenty-four year old man killed himself by laying down across the Union Pacific tracks a few blocks west of our house. There were fewer whistles, it seemed. I wondered if that wasn't my own projection, draping a kind of false mourning over northern Illinois. When I did hear a whistle cry, the thin peal sounded bewildered, breathless. The harmonies sung in each cry sounded to me like anxious conversation, lament. The trains appeared dazed, respectful; they moved slower on the tracks that afternoon. Their lights came on well before dusk, as if sweeping for bodies, the awful littering.

I wondered grimly on the details. The student was despondent over a romance. What a cliché. He'd warned his friends who had promptly called the local police, but they were too late. The man simply left his early-morning post as night manager at the local hotel, walked to the tracks and threw himself in front of a passing freight train. The train was slowing from 70 mph to the posted 50 mph when it struck him, but it is, as it turns out, nearly impossible for such a train to stop within a half mile. This had been the second time in a week that someone had committed suicide by throwing himself in front of a Union Pacific train. Only days before, a man in California had done the same thing.

I wonder if the ghosts of those killed by trains gather at the scenes and lament in an eerie threnody. Perhaps they celebrate. A roaring train through town is nearly an otherworldly specter, and maybe those who die by train expect deliverance, a blessing, a spiriting away from this world on a vehicle magnificent, heartbreaking, yet companionable in its loneliness, its flight through the unseen dark. *A ghost of a man carried in pieces toward the fabled sun idly scratches behind the ear of an animal's ghost, any animal's ghost whose dreadful instinct lifted him into the bright and black.*

Student Killed by Freight Train

While I sat on the log behind the Lincoln Inn Restaurant waiting for a train to come, I stared for nearly half an hour at a shimmering light a mile or so down the track. I rubbed my eyes but a light persisted, divine in its acuteness, a glow of faith. This light might have been what I wished it to be, a phantasm. Perhaps it was a flicker of the tumultuous past, a dire mistake made whole and bright again.

When I was an undergraduate student one of my favorite afternoon escapes from campus was to drive into Washington D.C., park somewhere off of upper Connecticut Avenue among the stately homes in Cleveland Park, and walk the broad street toward downtown. My favorite place, a few miles north of Dupont Circle at Calvert Street overlooking Rock Creek Park, was the Taft Bridge, a beautiful, impressive span bookended by two weathered, regal sculpted lions. From a spot halfway across the bridge I could look west toward Georgetown or back east toward Adams Morgan, and beneath me the traffic along Rock Creek Parkway skimmed silent along the floor of the city. The bridge—the highest, and one of the oldest, in the city—soared above plentiful, dark trees and the expansive Rock Creek riding stables, and I took solace in standing there.

Emboldened by something recklessly romantic, one day I climbed up onto the guardrail and swung my legs over. I was essentially floating above the park. If I looked just past the ends of my feet I could imagine that I was hovering, dreamlike, pure mood thrilling in the step from the known to the gusty. Within moments a passerby ran toward me.

"Don't! Don't do it. I promise you it's not worth it."

He reached me. "Let's talk about it," he said quietly, offering a hand.

This Must Be Where My Obsession With Infinity Began

Oh man this guy thinks I'm going to jump. Annoyed and embarrassed, I scrambled back over the rail to convince him that I had no intention of jumping. We had a brief pantomime of gestures and exclamations until he was sure that I wouldn't jump. I walked back over the bridge, a giant mural of Marilyn Monroe painted on the side of a pharmacy staring down at me, amused. I was self-conscious and peevish that this man could so melodramatically mistake my intention. How I must have looked to him! A young guy on a bridge, throwing it all away, for what? A girl? Poor grades? Parents who didn't love him?

Looking back, I see now that I was being reckless at a particularly reckless time. In the mid-eighties the Taft Bridge and its neighbor to the east, the Duke Ellington Bridge, were popular with suicide leapers, their fates luridly covered in the papers and made the stuff of urban legends. In 1986 the city erected "suicide girders" along the Ellington Bridge, much to the ire of citizens who ultimately took the local government to court on aesthetic grounds. But the girders remain there to this day, and in fact are the model for other cities wishing to forestall the indignity, and the mess, of death by leaping. As I straddled the Taft Bridge that afternoon the local controversy didn't involve me, and anyway I failed to appreciate the human dramatic dimensions of the suicides. I was a kid. I couldn't see the stencil for human tragedy that I had become to that thoughtful man on the bridge, the pain of self-annihilation as foreign and distant to me as the ground below.

An urban legend says that the machines that dominate our lives—personal computers, cash registers, data banks, etc.—give off an imperceptible white noise that is tuned, providentially, to a minor key. All around us, the metal-and-plastic boxes that promise so much are humming conspiratorially in a minor-key litany. Is this why I leave Wal-Mart so blue? Is this what I see in the dour looks of my students at the end of a long class beneath fluorescent lights, a kind of choral ennui that drains their faces and imagination of spirit? My own computer hums as I write this, as I try to navigate through the stubbornness of words a sense of what my imagination knows but cannot tell, of the sadness of train tracks before, and after, the trains.

I wonder if before the invention of movies we heard sentimental orchestral strings in our minds when we read sad passages in novels, or a wave of triumphant music when, say, little Sylvia perched atop the fir tree first spotted the prized heron's nest. In 1793 while a dying man gazed far ahead or far back in his imagination, did the edges of his perception grow poignantly fuzzy in a cinematic dreamscape? The men and women who scored the first films in Hollywood didn't create the soundtrack of our lives, they merely listened with well-tuned ears to the desperation of silent hours, when sadness and joy alike offer their strings to the world's bow. The symphonic swell that we are accustomed to hearing in film—accompanying two lovers' final embrace, or the unbearable stay at a young child's death bed—is sadly Platonic, a thin copy of a veiled orchestra that had finished tuning long before the world cooled, the baton first lifted millions of years ago when *grief* was not yet a word. I hear what can only be described as a low cello moan, sometimes barely audible, sometimes thrumming loudly in my throat. I hear in the vibrations a kind of music lost forever in the transparent day, scored and waiting for the lost to bow their heads and turn the sheet.

A couple of weeks after the suicide in my town I contacted John Bromley, the Director of Public Affairs for Union Pacific Railroad. I was interested in how often such events occur, how train operators deal with the incidents. How do they cope with being unwitting accomplices to a suicide? Are they trained for such grief?

Bromley answered me in an email: "Nationally on all U.S. railroads about 500 pedestrians trespassing on railroad property are killed by trains, slightly more than the 450 or so killed each year in train-auto collisions. Many of the pedestrian deaths are suicides, but we don't have a data base to identify them, as the final determinations of suicide are made by local authorities. At Union Pacific we have a peer-support group that train crews are referred to after fatal accidents. Train crews usually are relieved and replaced with another crew immediately after an accident, rather than completing their run."

Perhaps those haunted trains I imagined the day after the suicide were merely vessels for the sorrow inside of them, the grief of train operators whose concentration, buffed by daydreams of mortgages and spouses and box scores, was rudely interrupted by the severing of a human body. Bromley's answer was appropriately curt and officious, I thought. Why dwell on tragedy? And the tracks behind my house are hazy, gloomy now, and bereft.

The act of killing oneself intentionally: the dictionary definition is typically brusque—there are tens of thousands of other words to make room for, after all. A teacher of mine once claimed that the hardest sentence to write is one that begins with your name, and continues with the phrase, " . . . died today". And yet as I write the generic definition of suicide here, I find it also difficult, as if it's personal. I didn't know this student killed by a freight train, but his gesture enacts itself every day on the tracks behind my house, a hallucination at dusk on those early December afternoons when winter is up on its knees somewhere in the Arctic, filling its immense lungs.

"I, too, was suicidal once."

That sentence isn't difficult for me to write, because now that fact and the events surrounding that fact seem relatively trivial, remarkably shortsighted. I had, however, morphed (if tentatively) into a version of that guy on the bridge about to throw it all over. My egocentric moods at the time involved an overwrought relationship with Janet, a girl whom I had met the summer before college, and my inability to see beyond my own nose. (Ironically, she eventually moved into an apartment a few blocks north of the Taft Bridge). I lived many months in a kind of ponderous hysteria. Once I walked in a humid July night the three miles from my parents' house to Holy Cross Hospital, where I was born. Kneeling in the small, cool chapel for hours I prayed feverishly that my depression would lift. I prayed often that year, in Saint Andrew's the Apostle Church, where I had begun attending mass again (fitfully), between classes at the small white chapel at the leafy end of my college campus, and many more times in Holy Cross, where I took comfort in the nurses' squeaking shoes barely audible behind the chapel doors, their soft succor, and in the single, unwavering nun who seemed to be there around the clock, bobbing in her private dark and quiet.

Pushing my fists together until they whitened, I was desperate to shed my stubborn ego. I listened hopefully for answers. I remember once nodding my head uncertainly to my counselor at college who tried to explain my sadness away as an existential response to President Reagan's

This Must Be Where My Obsession With Infinity Began

emotionally vapid "Morning in America" election campaign from the year before. My counselor was a doctoral student in psychology, and I believe I was one of his field requirements. He was charmingly enthusiastic about his pet theory, which betrayed his liberal leanings and through which he hoped to filter every personal difficulty that I broached. My stomach bubbling with my standard midday meal (No-Doz and Dr. Pepper) I smiled and tried to agree with him, while inside a small voice brayed, an urgent but nameless tide of solipsism and dejection.

At the worst point I sat in the break room at the undergraduate library at the University of Maryland, slouched so willfully low that I felt I could have drained fluidly to the floor, breathlessly unhappy. I had been unable to thaw the scary freeze in my chest for months. *A ghost of a man carried in pieces toward the fabled sun.* I thought, *One way.* Luckily my fifteen minute break ended.

Years later I see myself unhappy on that hard plastic orange chair on the cracked linoleum floor under the harsh and ugly insistence of fluorescent lights in the basement of that library. I think of the student in my town. Buoyed on a swell of music only he heard, music so compelling as to feel like measured truth and counsel, he sat in a back office at Best Western and imagined with clinical precision the steps that he would take to the train tracks and his own, willful conclusion.

Yard Trauma

One guy we called *fetal pig*. He had a gimpy leg, stiffly cocked, one poor arm. He wore a platform shoe and thick glasses. The biology teacher screamed at us. That morning we drew shaking scalpels to the soft underside of a frog. I pinned thin skin-flaps to the table laying back its tiny dress. As taught, I sliced its stomach, drew it open. Inside lay a half-digested cricket, a stillness greater than that surrounding it. How abstract, the slow dissolve. This was many years ago.

But I can't get the formaldehyde out. Today, a curious circle of crow feathers in the back yard, some spearing the ground straight. Agony pulled though air. I walk outside to a crow dead in the yard, dropped from the tree like a handkerchief—closer: *that isn't a broken neck, or a head hid in a wing. That's a head cut clean off.*

What odd nature I live by.

This Must Be Where My Obsession With Infinity Began

God-Blurred World

This Must Be Where My Obsession With Infinity Began

The Innocents

Three hundred and seventy miles away, a camera photographs our own future: stars birthing, lucid suns, the dawn of fictions, constellations assembling slow narratives. One cloud is six trillion miles high, so high even a reckoning evaporates, so high that wind is a limb gone useless.

On earth, having alighted from a plane which had flown over the ivory heads of gods, I wondered aloud: "What really happened?" At home, I assembled a solar system in a shoebox. With kitchen string I made whole planets hover. The tiny Styrofoam ping-pong spheres rested in my palm—lesser God-land. Glued and pinned, a sun drawn in crayon.

Still later, driven along the edge of a thunderstorm (its measly cotton) I wondered at a god that plucks rain from the earth. *Should I be seeing this?* We can glimpse storm systems developing on planets light years away, I learned. And at the dinner table that night my mom was driven to despair when talk turned to infinity.

This Must Be Where My Obsession With Infinity Began

Abstracting My Dad

He was 11 or 12, the son of a day laborer, a little Italian kid browsing an oversized book about mathematics in his neighborhood public library in Williamsburg, Brooklyn. He paused at a page devoted to the Integral, and something about the curve of the classical form, the inscrutable but familiar nature of it, grabbed him. Fascinated, and in a kind of pre-teen bravado, he determined that one day he'd master the meaning of this math symbol. Fast forward: graduate school at Purdue University in West Lafayette, Indiana, and he's befuddled at the Wonder Bread placed on the table at the local Italian restaurant, but he'll find his studies engrossing, especially the math courses involving integral calculus. He'll soon get a job at IBM, and for decades will make wide use of integral calculus while working on NASA's unmanned scientific spacecraft program, with navigation, meteorology, astronomical, and earth-survey satellites, ballistic missile defense systems, telecommunication systems, highly-classified military intelligence systems, launch vehicle payload weight analysis and allocation, geosynchronous orbit analysis, system reliability analysis, and Global Positioning Satellites. He'd raise a family. Among his brood one son became a mathematics professor, one an engineer, one a telecommunications lawyer. And one who can't shake loose from his memory an abstract painting called *Broken Integral*.

I have five siblings. The moment my oldest brother was able to look after my youngest, my parents vaulted to a neighborhood restaurant, the first time they'd been out, alone, in years, and this became a weekly ritual that has lasted for decades. Sometimes while my parents were away, my older brothers and sister converted the basement into "Magic Night." Lowered fluorescent lights. A dramatically-thrown flashlight beam. Some eerie music playing from a scratchy LP. Home from the restaurant, my parents would be our audience, and *ooh* and *ahh* and clap with parental largess. A paint easel stood in a corner of the basement, and for one of the illusions, one of us would untie a coat hanger and secure one end around a paint brush while another would grip the other end and lurk behind the white-vinyl curtain that separated the basement from my dad's work space (One year, in what seemed to me like creating fire, he built a television set from a kit, the conjuring of a soldering iron, an oscilloscope, and some circuit boards.) Our invisible painter moved his brush back and forth across a propped canvas. We dubbed him "Vincent Van Gone." My parents duly applauded. I had to go to bed soon after.

More than a comic prop, this easel became a locus. Resting on it for many years was an odd, intense painting created by my dad, a lifetime mathematician, a man seduced and charmed by the ways of numbers, the hard, cruel circuit of spaceflight, and the objections of infinity. I've always been struck by the surreal sadness of the piece, originating as it did in a burst of inspiration. At IBM one afternoon, talking with my uncle about painting, my dad suddenly had the desire to paint. He rushed home—the image fully formed already—and put the composition together quickly. The lurid colors, the broiling, setting-sun vanishing point (I always see the sun setting, not rising), the tumbling Infinity symbol, the unmoored and wandering "O" at the bottom corner, the fractured Integral symbol itself: the mood is forcefully disturbed, and unhappy. My dad is not an unhappy man. For many years the contrasts between his temperamental conservatism and the bleakness of the painting, his love of numbers and systems and the curious content of this image, led to an unknown: my dad's shadowy, emotional life. An integral completes, forms a unit; his commingling of rational mathematics and irrational art-making, the rigidity of numerals and the wandering of the imagination, surprised and moved me.

"There are two worlds: the world we can measure with line and rule, and the world that we feel with our hearts and imagination," James Henry Leigh Hunt writes. "To be sensible of the truth of only one of these, is to know truth but by halves." Recently I asked my dad about the painting, and he confessed to me that he later decided that *Disenchantment* would have made for a more fitting title. *I guess the beauty, mystery, and intrigue of the integral faded over the years,* he said. Recently when I was in Williamsburg I looked for that book that he loved as a kid, but the library at Leonard and Devoe Streets had long been remodeled, re-shelved, re-catalogued. The book is gone.

This Must Be Where My Obsession With Infinity Began

The Sky's Tent

I was intrigued with my students whose dorm rooms were located in the convocation center, the large domed building at the south end of campus that housed residence rooms and basketball games alike. An apt metaphor for the yoking together of our daily domestic intimacies with the blared exaggerations of popular spectacle; as a culture we're getting so very loud and I wondered if my students could actually hear, from the safety of their own rooms, the boom of the PA announcer, the raucous cheers of the crowd, the anthem of Gary Glitter's "Rock & Roll (Pt. 2)" or the Ramones' "Blitzkrieg Bop."

The absolute object slightly turned is a metaphor of the object. (Wallace Stevens)

Or were the two environments hermetically sealed off from one another, the students floating through a kind of surreal stillness, aware that a few thousand people just like them were screaming dozens of feet away while they, in the quiet of their own rooms, brushed their teeth in their pajamas, thought of

This Must Be Where My Obsession With Infinity Began

their pets back home, of tomorrow's homework.

Years ago I stayed several days at the SkyDome Hotel (now Rogers Center), in Toronto. I knew that the dome housed the Toronto Blue Jays baseball team (and, at that time, the Toronto Raptors basketball team) and boasted an internationally-recognized hotel, and is recognized overall as one of the more prestigious venues in North America. I also knew that when Roberto Alomar was playing shortstop for the Blue Jays he lived in SkyDome, called it "home."

for my parents to leave me behind at the department store so that after closing I could pretend to sleep in any and all of the model beds and watch the dozens of television sets all at once and play house in the floor kitchens and leave thousands of industrial fluorescent lights blazing if I wanted to

When you imagine living in an undomesticated environment its intimacies slowly curl around you. In recent years when I'd watch the odd Blue Jays game on television I would scan just above upper-deck centerfield—in SkyDome this had metamorphosed into regal bay windows—for what I would guess was Alomar's room (his home) and wonder on the strange realities that he must have encountered groggily waking each morning inside a multi-sport entertainment complex.

Flying above the clouds at ten thousand feet in a jumbo jet you stare into God's blueprints. Driving alongside the edge of a thunderstorm thirty miles away from you, *this is something that shouldn't be allowed.*

When Amy and I arrived in our room at SkyDome I was

happy to find that it overlooked right field. But I wasn't prepared for how close I'd really be to the action. We peered out the window and discovered that the upper-deck seats ended, literally, a few feet beneath us. ("A fly-ball could so easily land nearby!" I exclaimed, stupidly.) We slid the windows open, stuck our heads out, inhaled the ageless aroma of peanuts: the fragrances of *buy me some peanuts and Cracker Jack* can be so efficiently transplanted into the climate-controlled, sealed environment of a late-century monolithic dome structure.

I dream of new-and-improved supermarket food-products. *Home-Cooked Style. Old-Fashioned Flavor.*

SkyDome's dome opens onto "true" climate: one of the world-famous attractions of this facility is its retractable roof. It takes twenty minutes to fully open, but eventually you're blessed with serene Canadian sunlight where before you'd suffered industrially-damned steel girders and paint. (Under the sun, a ballgame's perfume ages to Wrigley Field-vintage.) None of this mattered much in late-December at SkyDome. The baseball season had long since ended and the Raptors, disappointingly, were out West somewhere on a road trip. From our room, the bird's-eye entertainment spectacle we were granted access to was *Walt Disney's Beauty and the Beast on Ice*.

Fears that we wouldn't actually be able to see this Disney miracle, however, were soon satisfied. From the vantage point of our window all we saw were the tops of colossal navy-blue curtains, draped extravagantly and somewhat messily over an entire half of the SkyDome arena. It looked as though something furtive and hushed was going on

This Must Be Where My Obsession With Infinity Began

beneath us, something for which we hadn't the clout nor the cash to witness. From our room the whole production looked slap-dash. If it weren't for the lobby posters announcing the event and for the odd, muffled roar of the pageant's canned score (imagine hearing a piece of music from the *inside* of your body first, and then out through your ears) we wouldn't know anything was going on beneath us that was worth the price of admission.

Nothing dissolves mystery quicker—raining down disappointment, fear, dissolution—than spying the inner workings, machinations, the click-and-the-whir. This is why house-facades—the appearance of a comfortable home, the likes of which one sees propped up at new housing developments, or lining "Main Street USA" at any number of amusement parks—are sad. To a child, to discover simple wooden beams supporting an exterior that one believed was a home in all of its safe and nurturing intimacy was shocking. And gloomy. *Verisimilitude* comes from Latin: "very similar." I learned the pity of adverbs pretty early.

It turns out that what I amateurishly considered "curtains" was in fact "SkyTent Arena." Lay ignorance cured by the room brochure, I soon learned that SkyTent Arena "is an acoustical system which completely encloses one section of SkyDome creating an intimate arena. With movable sides and an adjustable roof, SkyTent allows for a flexible seating capacity from 10,000 to 30,000." They admire adjustable roofs around here, which is all well and good except that from our room all we saw was the outside of a tent, not the luxurious interior housing all kind of spectacle. Obviously this made sense, as we hadn't paid to see *Walt Disney's Beauty and the*

Beast on Ice and didn't honestly expect an opportunity to watch it from the room—nonetheless the whole experience soon became odd and unsettling. The dim music, the muted applause (all while applying deodorant in your room) lent a surreal feeling to our stay at SkyDome, underscored by our view: here we saw the backs of everything, as if we had been escorted into a place that we shouldn't have been.

The magician pulls scarf after scarf of breathtaking colors from the single white handkerchief. The children squeal, learning bounty, and faith. After the show the local insurance adjustor bends over his box of tricks. A fake, faintly-grotesque thumb drops from his vest pocket. He sighs.

The invisible. The necessary. Duende, the inscrutable, the pervasive secret at the core. "These 'dark sounds' are the mystery," Federico Garcia Lorca writes, "the roots thrusting into the fertile loam known to all of us, ignored by all of us, but from which we get what is real in art. [Manuel] Torres here agrees with Goethe who defined the duende when he attributed to Paganini 'a mysterious power that everyone feels but that no philosopher has explained.'" Later, Lorca calls duende "the spirit of the earth."

From my room at SkyDome I watch gloomily as characters from *Beauty and The Beast* waddle off of the stage into the backstage dressing-area. The murky applause and hyped voice of the PA announcer do nothing to imbue these creatures with grace.

    The teapot, having been lifted by a few burly stevedores, inelegantly drops to the floor. The candlesticks, awkwardly lumbering about, bump into each other. Slowly they peel off

This Must Be Where My Obsession With Infinity Began

their costumes, and what remains: sweaty adults in tights with their hair sticking straight up. Shoulders sag; they're exhausted. Production assistants and stagehands scurry about, helping the dancers out of costumes, wiping away makeup. The anthropomorphism of a teapot into the suddenly human: this person has a car to drive home, bills to pay, a spouse to love, to placate.

A magic trick: something extraordinary happens during, and inside, this brief arrangement of words and sounds, but it all remains invisible. Try as hard as you might, you cannot pinpoint with exact precision how James Wright, at the end of "Autumn Begins in Martins Ferry, Ohio," arrives at:

> Therefore,
> Their sons grow suicidally beautiful
> At the beginning of October,
> And gallop terribly against each other's bodies.

Little in the poem prepares the reader for the miraculous and stunning—the magical—transformation, out under the lights at a trivial high school football game, of those adolescents into desperate beasts kicking up their heels at their fates. I've read this poem a hundred times: I'm always astonished. Where's the "on" switch. Metaphor as a "carrying over"—but from what to what? We remain unmoored, and a bridge is shaped from the invisible to the invisible.

One gift of art: it withholds its secrets. I can't flip Wright's poem on its back, take it apart, first undoing tiny screws, then removing the outer lid, and then the assembly, spreading its contents out on the desk. When you flip a poem over, out of

The Sky's Tent

respect or out of insolence, you remain with the poem only. Contents drift covertly around you in the mist of discovery. There are no insides we can see. No strings attached.

Sleepless at three in the morning, lured by the queer stilling of wonder beneath me, I get up and look out the window, solitary in the immense, dormant SkyDome. I'm jarred by the sight of a dozen or so small children lined up against the backstage wall, motionless, as if in suspension. Their tiny heads are down—they're waiting in glum anticipation for the next show? When my eyes adjust to the dark I realize: these aren't children, they're the tiny, empty costumes of the spoons and forks, leaning in abeyance.

A priest looms large, nearly transparent. In his hands he caresses transubstantiation. We are grateful in its presence.

A server sitting next to a priest at the altar, startled into attention by the priest's furtive, side-mouth request: *count the parishioners' heads, we need a count for the dioceses, we gotta fill this place, ya know.*

Toto, pulling aside the curtain.

They never turn the lights off at SkyDome. We had to pull a chair up against our room curtains to ensure darkness for sleep. That absurd cutlery below, the otherworldly glare.

Stumbling on your naked mother in the bathroom as she bends over, her damp back to you.

You can kill a magician from fright by surprising him from behind.

This Must Be Where My Obsession With Infinity Began

Customized Environmental Sound Machine

In Georges de La Tour's *The Repentant Magdalene*, painted more than three hundred years ago, a plain woman in a loose-fitting robe sits at her desk, one hand holding her resting head—she's large with thought—the other hand touching a skull, as if reading a kind of braille. The skull obscures a candle or a gas lamp; it lights the face of this woman, as if knowledge is a slow-moving front of burning light, settling its warmth-in-darkness as afterthought. The woman drifts and I wonder less on her sins or her meditation than on her coming to be: de La Tour's oils buff and buff the canvas as if rubbing to a source, loving what it finds. The dark pigments circle the center of the canvas where the flame resides, where the skull interrupts, where our eyes drift hungry for the middle, for truth. The dark is nearly all there is but for the gentle sway of the flame licking its way into consciousness.

This is about the body and time. How many drafts and how many hours de La Tour lived before this form of the world agreed through desire and thought to come. How de La Tour learned the round world comes moment upon

This Must Be Where My Obsession With Infinity Began

moment until a month goes, until a year drains from the muscles, until it is ready to breed lust and idea.

Driving along US 90 I steer my car between white lines—a kind of discipline, a kind of knowledge—past skeletons of desire-into-form. If you blink you miss a building sprouting up so fast that the jets aiming their progress across time's skies have to dodge them. This is a crowded place we breathe in, the dimensions of living flattening around us into bright color and noise. Stilled in an endless line of locomotion I see around me all sorts of bodies tuning in their radios for urban warmth of information, sighing behind hands propping up heads already sounding toward skulls. Brief flickers of reflection stopped as time speeds itself thin.

The God-Blurred World

Recently I looked at newspaper coverage of the 1969 Apollo 11 lunar mission: front page after front page of banner headlines, screaming two-inch type, giddy editorial cartoons, all reported manner of visionary enthusiasm and tearful astonishment for a new future where moon creatures have been disproved and NASA will rescue us all. Writer and sci-fi visionary Ray Bradbury wanted to create a new calendar, beginning with "Year One of the New Era."

In Section One, on page two of the July 20, 1969 edition of the *Chicago Tribune*—barely noticeable in the lower-left corner, the insubstantial pica-width dwarfed to near extinction by the booster power of Apollo media coverage—ran a small item:

Mother Kills Self and Two Children
Millstone, N.J., July 19 (AP)—Mrs. Nancy A. Schnitzer, 29, killed her children Douglas Jr., 9, and Donna Lynn, 2, with a 12-gauge shotgun and then turned the weapon on herself at the Schnitzer home here, police said.

This Must Be Where My Obsession With Infinity Began

A headline near the top of that page read "Here's Scenario for 1st Moonwalk!" But beneath was documented proof that what gripped much of a world barely penetrated the appalling consciousness of one house in New Jersey.

As a kid, I loved watching the television footage of the Saturn V and Apollo rockets lifting off from Cape Canaveral: the otherworldly orange of the heat and flame, the intense, God-awful vapors. I glimpsed the inside of a universe—a dream, a hell—that I'd never before seen. The attached scaffolding and ladders on the launch pad, surreal in its height of three hundred and sixty-three feet, fell away like so much lint as we struggled to master gravity while three hundred pounds of monomethylhydrazine fuel and nitrogen tetroxide oxidizer, 41,000 pounds of engine propellants firing to make lunar orbit insertion, and the coral glow of the booster rockets all lit a world new again. Such backlit *mise-en-scène*. If the image-art of cinema offered this century not merely verisimilitude but indeed a new way of seeing the world and ourselves, then the liftoff blazes that enkindled southern Florida in the late-Sixties and early-Seventies were also atomic filters of a new frontier, lighting the antiques below.

The Stations of the Cross were welcome respite from the unexciting certainties of the classroom. For many of us grade school kids at Saint Andrew the Apostle there was a cinematic drama in this Act of Contrition describing Christ's final day on earth, unlike any other religious service. Church always held for me an overpowering theatrics. The grave silence bespoke a story in progress: entering church, I always felt as if I were entering a movie in the middle. It was a story I felt left out of many times. The bored faces of my classmates suggested that they, too, had missed the climax.

Were we too young? Too inattentive? We had to listen hard for legend.

I absorbed a great deal about the art of narrative from attending church. The bible readings and gospels were full of stories suffused with imagery, their fragments arching into a kind of cohesion: the pantomime of Easter; the stripping down of the altar during Lent; the slender green palms we brought home to hang, drooping and ignored, in the kitchen.

Weekly worshiping had become rote and tired, and so I looked forward to Stations of the Cross with the keenest interest; there was a dignity and spiritual heft to the ritual that seemed absent on Sundays. The Stations were unpredictably observed: I didn't know when, or why, we'd head down in single-file to the building annexed to our classroom wing. As we marched, the usual dread of the gloom-tainted church and of tense playground politics that manifested themselves even in the house of God, when with whom you sat could make or break an afternoon, dissipated, lifted into something grand.

I'd heard the narrative of the crucifixion told often, was no longer riveted by Golgotha and The Shroud. Rather, the deep pleasure of Stations was something closer to the warmth and bodily enchantment I experienced during "reading time," the late-afternoon classroom diversion during which Sister Nena would ask us to lay our heads down on our desktops as she'd read to us from an oversized storybook. What luxury! My formica desktop would moisten with my breath's nearness. Plot didn't much matter; it was her telling that enveloped me. When Sister would interrupt the tale to speak to someone at the classroom door I'd have to wait, in a kind of suspension, half-drowsy, half-attentive, for the story to resume, her voice

This Must Be Where My Obsession With Infinity Began

to again fill my small head with perfume. Afterwards I'd feel dizzy, and would resume my normal classroom activities in a kind of haze: surely this had as much to do with the sleepiness that the activity was designed to induce in rambunctious ten-year-olds as it had to do with a depth in myself that I felt had been reached by the story. Sister Nena's reading time and the stories of the Stations of the Cross are linked in a timeless fabric, which, as a boy, I pulled over me in a darkness of myth.

    I haven't attended a Stations of the Cross service in years. Memories revolve around that grade-school boy who felt compelled to listen less by burden than by desire. As they are in most Catholic churches, the fourteen Stations were arranged along the side aisles at Saint Andrew, each story-fragment of Christ's final afternoon manifested in an etching hanging on the wall. A church's sweeping immersion of itself—and of its parishioners—into the arts was a magnificent introduction for me to a fundamental aspiration, the translation of the untranslatable. Church involves a panorama of the aural, the written, the theatrical, the visual, the plastic arts, which all nearly overwhelmed my nascent senses. The incense wafting into my lungs during Sunday's High Holy Mass entered me not as the Spirit of God, but as the Spirit of Story.

    For me, then, the great churches existed in an erotics of representation, pulsing as much with art's invisible desire to make manifest the splendor of our chaotic world, as with the Holy Spirit's desire to make itself manifest in our chaotic selves.

    Characteristic of most devotional exercises, the fourteen Stations of the Cross demand a rigor of the body, a pious severity echoed in the harsh pews, the hush of the service, the rigid formulae of the idiom. And the meditative pause at each image for prayer and consideration reflected not simply the severity of Christ's suffering but the immensity of the image's power as a narrative. Though our heads were down in our prayer books, our imaginations wandered through the artful constructions of each picture. The etchings at Saint Andrew weren't extraordinary in any respect, being Sixties-style generic reliefs of dark-brown wood and shiny, gold-tinted metal. But that didn't matter: the shape constancy of Christ's agony and sacrifice wrought by each pose attracted me. The desire for spirit made manifest in the physical realm was all too apparent to me as a young boy gazing upward at a thin man, his head hung in anguish beneath exhausted shoulders, forced to carry a cross after having fallen for a third time. Such pictures gripped me, and bred in me an appreciation for the power and durability of the narrative image. Saint Andrew's, I marvelled, was as much a Church of Art as a Church of Worship.

And the stories accrue. Each of the individual Stations is horrific, abhorrent: Jesus condemned to Death; Jesus bears His Cross; Jesus Christ crucified; Jesus falls; Jesus stripped of His garments and given gall to drink . . . . The horror was echoed even in those stories which reflected relative moments of surcease. When Simon of Cyrene helps Jesus to carry the cross, when Veronica wipes his face with cloth, even the moment when Jesus meets his holy mother are merely pauses in a gruesome narrative, a cinematic detail akin to the clock on the wall ticking louder if we dare to ignore its power in our fateful affairs.

Regardless of my own beliefs and my own doubts, which are

unimportant in this connection, it is my own opinion that art lost its basic creative drive the moment it was separated from worship. It severed an umbilical cord and now lives its own sterile life, generating and regenerating itself. In former days the artist remained unknown and his work was to the glory of God. He lived and died without being more or less important than other artisans; "eternal values," "immortality" and "masterpiece" were terms not applicable in his case. The ability to create was a gift. In such a world flourished invulnerable assurance and natural humility, Ingmar Bergman

The etchings at Saint Andrew's embodied worship, striving to incarnate the common and drab insults waged against Christ's mortal body. That these illustrations hung in a church and not in a museum suggested that I focus on dogma. "The artist considers his isolation, his subjectivity, his individualism almost holy," Bergman laments, and in my burgeoning artistic sensibility I found that I wanted a kind of aesthetic of worship that reconciled doctrine with engraving, creed with brushstroke. I couldn't articulate this at the time, of course. I think that my article of faith issued as much from my gaping response to the sublime of creative, artistic representation as from the sublime of Christ's spiritual agony.

In what did I truly (want to) believe? If these pictures hung in the immense darkness of my church? If these pictures held themselves together against disorder to tell a story? The fragments of Christ's final day assembled themselves into a narrative so true that when I left church, blinking and sneezing in the banal sunlight, I lifted my eyes and saw wholeness.

When I became an altar server I quietly hoped that my

immersion in the spiritual drama of church would somehow intensify. I don't attempt here to diminish the effect that serving mass had on me as a young boy. It tattooed me with compelling memories and worthy reflection. But I can't deny that the experience—as appropriate as this seems to me now, many years later—was an unsolicited introduction to bureaucracy and backstage machinations. The first time I entered the sacristy I expected something akin to Wallace Stevens' "holy hush of ancient sacrifice," a kind of exotic portal of sacred vessels and vestments. What I saw first was a flimsy calendar hanging on a wall, dates circled hastily in red ink. There were fluorescent tubes and cardboard boxes stacked unceremoniously onto wobbling, cramped shelves. Communion wafers, pre-Consecration, waited in drab plastic bags, like materials for a classroom experiment. The first time I served with older boys, the frank and secular tone of their conversations—we were, after all, preteens—shocked me a little. Our sneakers squeaked on the sacristy floor as at a gym. It felt like a back room. I hadn't expected that God needed a mini refrigerator to keep His wine well.

Despite these small disappointments, I looked forward to assisting the priest during the Stations. In this Act, the server's role is modest. He (or she, as quickly became the case at Saint Andrew) is either the cross-bearer or the acolyte. I recall being assigned the latter duty more often, but I would often stare into the candle's flame in exaggerated apathy. My languor surprised me: I'd hoped that serving would enrich and deepen my attraction to the Stations, but, though I now recollect them amusingly, the stage-directions barked at me by various priests both frightened me and deromanticized the passion of the service, reducing it to another theatrical event.

This Must Be Where My Obsession With Infinity Began

Ultimately, what my distancing from the Stations of the Cross, what my ennui led to was a fascination for stories left *untold*. I see this now as the beginnings of my fascination with the marginal and the shadowed. In a kind of aesthetic democracy I began wondering about the lives of those people unrepresented in the Stations' etchings. Surely their lives didn't matter as much as the Son of God's and yet, I asked myself during one particular service late in my precocious dissatisfactions, weren't their lives the very lives He died for, the very lives so graced and enriched by His agony and sacrifice? Whither went the dirt and pebbles swept from the temple floor? I wondered how many dignified faces disappeared slowly from the early drafts of the Stations narratives.

My proposal is that Jesus' first followers knew almost nothing whatsoever about the details of his crucifixion, death, or burial. What we have now in those detailed passion accounts is not history remembered but prophecy historicized. And it is necessary to be very clear on what I mean here by prophecy. I do not mean texts, events, or persons that predicted or foreshadowed the future, that projected themselves forward toward a distant fulfillment. I mean such units sought out backward, as it were, sought out after the events of Jesus' life were already known and his followers declared that texts from the Hebrew Scriptures had been written with him in mind. Prophecy, in this sense, is known after rather than before the fact, John Dominic Crossan, Jesus: A Revolutionary Biography

The passion narratives of Jesus were constructed more than a half-century after his death. Prophesied backwards as Crossan suggests, the figure of Jesus grew in stature. His grace ennobling him into a kind of ur-reality, it is only fitting that the unknown, the ordinary around him, fell away. Though the canvas of redemption is an infinite canvas, stretching over a Zion horizon, it is also in some ways finite, a product of this world, painted by humans with revisionist strokes. Naturally, as the drafts proceeded, much commonplace history fell away.

The Stations of the Cross ask us to see Jesus as a slowly dying man whose spirit strengthens beneath the lash. The Stations also ask that we see Jesus as emblematic, as all of man. The Schnitzer household in Millwood, New Jersey, littered with the remains of three lives too scarred to be lifted, went scarcely noticed on the day of the Apollo wonder, the day Ray Bradbury, in his consecration of lunar culture, offered "The First Day of the Dawn Calendar of the New Era." Surely on Christ's final mortal day there were countless individual dramas enacting themselves near Nazareth, near Bethlehem, near Bethany, dramas which, in the boundaries of their own daily, but infinite concerns, enacted lives utterly important. W.H. Auden witnesses those everymen, who by the end of the poem will have to move on, in the opening lines of "Musée des Beaux Arts":

> About suffering they were never wrong,
> The Old Masters: how well they understood
> Its human position; how it takes place
> While someone else is eating or opening a window or
>   just walking dully along . . .

There they are. Though the images of the Stations edit out the men and women who witnessed the crucifixion,

This Must Be Where My Obsession With Infinity Began

foregrounding the mystery, the enactment of the Stations is a call to remember our very humanness, as mystery competes with fleshly suffering for our attention.

During the Stations services, my imagination wandered into the lives of those forgotten, and I wandered down the stony paths behind the buildings which lined the road toward the Place of the Skull. A kind of Passion for the Apocryphal, this fascination on my part reached zenith levels during particular services and at times I was prodded by the peevish priest to move forward to the next Station. Beneath the continental cloud of the crucifixion drama moved a mass of humanity that I dreamed about in head-tingling rapture. Who are these people? What *are* their lives? What was in the trash heaps. What did a ravenous Roman eat for breakfast that morning. Did the trees bloom. Crossan quotes Martin Hengel reminding us that "[c]rucifixion as a penalty was remarkably widespread in antiquity . . . it was, of course, carried out publicly"—I recalled that some Stations pictures I had studied in books portrayed Roman citizens in the trees, watching the crucifixion as a spectacle. What did they wear? How well did their sandals fit? Which small children played in the dirt and sand a game of their imaginations, distracted by the high sun? Which citizens were uninterested in the drama? Was that one there shamefully newly pregnant, her consciousness fixed inconsolably on the spirit inside of her? Wasn't there one man lying in his bed upstairs, belching and absently rubbing his stomach? Who turned their backs, and why?

That one over there, was his heart broken? My cinematic mind's-eye panned any imagined crowd scene, training itself on the unremarkable, zooming in on the backs of buildings, searching for imperfections in architecture and construction, building a new vista for my increasingly secular imagination that could not help but wonder about the lives of these narratively forsaken.

This Must Be Where My Obsession With Infinity Began

Occasional Prayer

You pray in your distress and in your need; would that you might also pray in the fullness of your joy and in your days of abundance, Kahlil Gibran

She asks for quiet. I merge the car onto the tollway, balancing a cup of McDonald's coffee between my legs. Our little ritual. We'll place the cups in their cardboard tray and, during the first mile or so, each say a quiet prayer, for safety, for ours and others'. Mine will be a simple request. A statement, really. (*Please watch over us and see that we arrive safely from our destination to our destination please watch over all drivers and pedestrians and see that each and every one arrive safely from their destination to their destination.*) In my best cultural Catholicism this will be followed by a mumbled Lord's Prayer. I'll labor to concentrate while I pray, elbowing out pesky grammarian voices. Amy always takes a little longer, gazing at passing fields. Her Jewish entreaties are longer and more involved. Complex, anyway. ("I have more people to say hi to," she'll shrug later.) Before long I'm eyeing my coffee, idly thinking that I'll check Wikipedia

This Must Be Where My Obsession With Infinity Began

when we get back home and read up on those Coffee Burning Lawsuits. Real? Urban Myth? Anyway, I'm impatient to drink.

The routine and self-centeredness that quickly wove itself into praying when I was young is a fact of my spiritual life that I've often wondered about, sensing that it must mean something, suggest a larger understanding of the worthiness of a life lived in conscious struggle. When I fell away from the church in my late-teens, I fell as a cliché. Burdened at an early age with hyper self-consciousness, I'd be overly-aware while at mass at Saint Andrew the Apostle, gripped in the classic adolescent manner by doubts and anxieties: *Am I getting it?* What "it" was I didn't know, only that the stern frowns of the nuns that I imagined turned toward me while I struggled to focus on prayer felt like a facial equivalent of a check-minus.

When I was ten or eleven years old I was convinced that my family was trying to kill me. Each night I'd lean over the bathroom sink down the hall from the bedroom I shared with my younger brother, trembling as I brushed my teeth, knowing for certain—the certainty being the splash of cold fear in my chest—that my older brothers, conniving with my parents, had poisoned the Crest with venom hidden in the basement. I'd lie in bed later, next to my younger brother, and stare at the dark ceiling in slow, crawling dread that I'd within minutes begin the agonizing writhe into death. My sibings' jackal, wild-eyed faces hovered over me in the dark, I'd hear conspiratorial muttering in the hallway, quiet smiling. Eventually, my fears blossomed to include poisoned breakfasts, lunches, dinners, snacks, all manner of household *terreur cuisine.*

A couple of years later I was locked in chest-tightening blues in seventh grade, convinced that my friends hated me and wanted me to disappear. In my imagination I was plagued by boys who yapped at each other in a foreign language and with girls with blossoming breasts who looked right through me. I'd wander to the other side of Saint Andrews, and stand mutely and pathetically by a pole and its flopping flag. I confessed this all to my mom on a long night when she found me sobbing hysterically in the shower, Faberge Organic shampoo running down my face. Moments later she slapped me. It's testament to the relationship I have with my mom that I understood the desperation behind the gesture: her son was turning into a self-obsessed monster, *Get out of yourself already!* I had a small bruise to lie about the next day, though I don't think that anyone noticed. Within a couple of weeks, the depression lifted. I was social again.

I never confessed to my family my irrational fears that they were trying to dispose of me—instead, I prayed. Staring into darkness, I'd clasp my hands and mutter pleas to the ceiling. By morning, waking bittersweetly to the chirpings of blackbirds and the roar of a Ride-On bus outside my window, the fear was gone but the memory would wash over me, leaving a faint ink-stain. Of course, soon enough this paranoia lifted for good, replaced by another comic opera courtesy of puberty, but I'm not so sure that I'll ever understand. My response to a fundamental dread was to reach for words that might somehow haul me above the lousy bedroom and my own manufactured dread.

I returned to praying fervently when I was in college. I'd met my girlfriend Janet the summer after high school; we both had worked at Baskin Robbins, forging a kind of acne-scarred bunker mentality, our wrists heroically weary, arms tattooed in Chocolate Almond and Daiquiri Ice. Looking

This Must Be Where My Obsession With Infinity Began

back at the relationship unraveling painfully over the next several years, I wonder why I didn't end it sooner. Most of the hysteria was the age-appropriate melodrama particular to liberal arts majors convinced that they discovered the irony of thrift store clothes-shopping, and who spent hours on the phone lamenting the distance and the failure of language to translate the exquisite experience of Being In Love! Etcetera. (I learned the word *egocentric* from my mom, who'd mutter it under her breath while passing by me—curled up on a chair near the phone, receiver in hand—as she calculated extravagant phone bills.) Now: I see a nineteen-year old kid in over his head, flirting with girls in his Romantic Lit class, comparing his girlfriend's butt and thighs to theirs, longing for a hickey and a secret smile from a new girl. Janet and I became too involved, too soon, and I had too big a heart (or too puny the courage) to break up with her and to get drunk with new girls snug in tight jeans and leg warmers in the loud, sticky bars along Route One in College Park. Even if I silently deplored the fashion choices of the girls I sat next to (I was too ironic for anything but Thrift Shop Chic) I longed to lie on a couch with them and unbutton their Calvin Klein off-the-rack color-block blouses and tug down their acid-washed, casually-torn Guess jeans.

After college I moved away to southeast Ohio to begin graduate school. I was untethered from Janet and our mutual friends, and began my semi-dedicated career as a drinker and serial womanizer, knowing that even lost in rum hangovers sweetened by patchouli oil, kiss-sore lips, and a new, bright-eyed girls' bra and panties under my bed, Janet's heart was a large and generous, if frightfully naïve and kind, heart that really, really, didn't deserve this. I stayed with her and carried inside of my chest a nervous chill that lasted for years.

I had dreams wherein I pleaded to surgeons with shadows for faces to cut open the front of me and remove this pulpy mass of nerves, which I visualized as a kind of cancerous lump. I was clearly depressed, not only in the existential way that so many twenty-something's are, burdened by a future grimly promising that the value and currency of pure sensation and of matters of the heart will diminish in the face of pricey, looming adulthood. I was twisted by the growing unhappiness with my girlfriend wrestling with a somewhat absurd, gallant notion of doing the right thing and staying with her, she the She of Such Great Promise only the year before.

One windy fall day I was moving across campus between classes (or, more likely, during classes) I looked up from my self-centered stupor. There: the fresh, blinding white of Memorial Chapel. I entered into the calm and the quiet—two states-of-being foreign to me in college—and the clean, bracing woodsy smell of pew-and-altar that brought me back to childhood. Leaving bright sunshine, the politics of the classrooms and cafeteria, the swell of humanity behind me, I discovered in the chapel a cool silence that compelled me to face a couple of things, though I wasn't articulating this to myself with clarity at age 20:

One: quiet contemplation and prayer forces you to engage yourself, to self-interrogate.

Two: God am I self-absorbed. Invariably my prayers revolved around one entity, the most all-encompassing being in the universe.

So, I took to praying. The odd Sunday, alone or with family, that I'd begun to again attend mass became, well, a religious experience. The period I looked forward to the most during

This Must Be Where My Obsession With Infinity Began

services was after Eucharist when I'd return to the pew and kneel in silence, press my hands together so tight that they'd whiten, and focus so intensely on saying the Lord's Prayer that I felt as if I'd become invisible to myself (my chief and most fervent wish ever since adolescence). Next to me, my bored brother would turn and make some sarcastic crack—our usual sacramental pastime—but then notice my eyes shut tight, my brow furrowed, my lips moving. He'd back off, curious and annoyed with me that I'd embarrassed him for intruding, for sabotaging our churchly gossiping. I was curious, too: about this new-found capacity to leave behind daily dread by focusing on prayer—or more accurately on the pleasure of words, on the satisfying sibilants slithering around my mouth. I thought that I understood meditation in these moments, the elemental release of all things material, the phrase *lead us not into temptation* becoming a mantra for me and an especially meaningful one, as a kind of chanted talisman to ward off not only sexual holds but—I realize now—the temptation to surrender to myself and to my self's obnoxious, noxious indulgences. I was addicted to Joe, and the temptations were too great.

My occasional prayer finds me less reaching a higher state, than desperately shedding ego. Perhaps this explains my impulse to write autobiographically. Does self-addiction wiggle from its straitjacket by turning outward to others in an attempt to make larger humane sense? And I wonder, can I pray for that. *Prayer does not change God*, writes Kierkegaard, *but changes him who prays.*

One clammy, bug-drenched night I staggered out of my house into the early dark, pointed surely if aimlessly down the street. Within a block I knew what I wanted: to pray and

Occasional Prayer

to leave myself behind. I headed toward Georgia Avenue, the main, busy thoroughfare through Wheaton, and turned south toward Holy Cross Hospital. Two and a half miles later I arrived, damp, knifed into the air-conditioned coolness of the hospital lobby, and made a quick right toward the chapel. I was customarily pleased to learn that the chapel door was open—is always open—and I took a seat in a middle pew. I took note of the two other people there: an anonymous supplicant, a mother, perhaps, praying for a child or another loved one; and a nun, always a nun, bobbing her head in sacred solitude.

There's great, if unusual, comfort in praying in the chapel at the very hospital where one had been born decades before, somewhere upstairs. The utter care into which I'd been delivered, the weight of the years behind me: these sensations were intensified as, catching my breath, I settled into the growing serenity of public prayer. Most appealing—indeed, at the time, what was necessary for me—was the buoyancy, as if shutting eyes tight and clasping hands together acted as a kind of sealant, trapping inside of me a consecrated lightlessness, a vapor that would slowly lift me from myself. Beyond this: the sad counterweight of my body—that sweating thing—tethered to the ground where girlfriends, flirtatious eyes, and other major nuisances prowled. If I'd open my eyes or unclasp my hands, the helium would release. And down to the world I'd go.

Christ encourages private prayer. Matthew 6:5-7:
> But when you pray, go into your room, close the door and pray to your Father, who is unseen. Then your Father, who sees what is done in secret, will reward you. And when you pray, do not keep on

babbling like pagans, for they think they will be heard because of their many words.

The mind is a large house with many rooms. The rooms are connected—by hallways, by frayed runners, by wall lamps, by desire and by memories. One can seal off a room—a child has moved to college, say, or a mother has expired in the back, or mites have infested the front—but that room remains, a tattoo on those who live and have lived there, indelible. And: guests enter the house through the grand rooms, not through the dank basement, the newspaper-strewn back porch, or descending from a musty attic. Yet those ignored rooms remain there, dark, and tissued to other rooms.

The mind is a large house with many rooms. We box up and store away what embarrasses and confounds us. Our boxes of pornography, our caches of candy bars, our booze, our rubber-banded letters from ex-boyfriends, ex-girlfriends, lost sons and daughters. Boxes remain and rooms remain and we remain in those rooms though we wish the rooms away.

I don't think that this is what Christ intends when he calls Apostle Peter to be the rock foundation on which He would build the church: to construct on that rock a large house with many rooms. Because into a room of my choice I can safely store prayer away in a box that I hurry to, or that I ignore. Can praying be compartmentalized and stacked next to the *Battleship* board game I blow dust off of when I'm feeling nostalgic? And yet. Too often it is easy to simply close the door behind me after praying, the thrown light-switch a darkened synapse gap that widens, stranding me further from prayer as a daily necessity, a daily faith. Muttering in a dark room and then blinking into a front foyer's light: Am I really in the same house?

Occasional Prayer

Here's Auden again, a convert to Christianity, a man with sin in his DNA: "To pray is to pay attention to something or someone other than oneself. Whenever a man so concentrates his attention—on a landscape, a poem, a geometrical problem, an idol, or the True God—that he completely forgets his own ego and desires, he is praying." My incessant mental taps on my own shoulder drew attention away from friends, family, work, and toward myself and the growing universe at which I was the center, the ends of my fingertips resting at the furthest, incomprehensible cosmos. But I was tired of being my own god. Gandhi writes that "Prayer is not asking. It is a longing of the soul. It is daily admission of one's weakness." OK, I was longing to be rid of myself, admitting to the weakness that was my own (*in media res*) biography: I was young, my brain was still developing (I write, to let myself off easy). But I'm displeased with these particular urges to prayer. The origin of most of the appeals I've muttered in my life has been either compulsory or egotistical, *Catechism* or *Bonomo*. This is a trait of the deeply egocentric man. If I long while praying, in the Ghandi manner, it's usually a longing for a kind of anonymity, a draining of the nasty details of my personality. I can't ignore the fundamental selfishness there too, that what I often pray for is a release of my own pettiness, shallowness, immaturity. (Prayer as self-help.) What do I, a man with nearly five decades behind him, pray for? The health of my family. The ease of destructive, irrational global politics. But more frequently: that the White Sox will bring the tying runner home from third. That the DVD+r discs will format. That the new stack laundry unit will fit in the pre-existing space. I know: few of us have Gandhi's transcendent will and selflessness. Didn't he lie next to a luscious naked girl one long night of the soul to test his celibacy? Or is that an apocryphal story. In my Seventeenth century lit class I might've felt Gandhi-like steeling myself next to the girl who I wanted to bend over the desk. But, really.

Amy and I are back from our drive later, and I'll repeat to myself what she'd said in the car when I'd asked her why her prayers are longer than mine. *More people to say hello to.* More people to stretch toward on the thin prop of prayer. More to caress *in absentia*, to tap lovingly on a shoulder knowing that touch is a foreign language, not spoken here. There. And I'll wonder, who do I have to say hello to? Who do I have to surprise, moist-eyed, my mouth moving oddly, slowly, the other tilting his head tenderly to make out the words. Alone to myself in my room, my words perish on the mirror.

In grade school, during required services, the soft rain beyond the stained glass windows puddling in a grayness at my center that I couldn't comprehend; in adolescence, during Holy Week services with my family, absently running fingers over mountainous acne and recoiling from the sound of my own ugly, monotonous voice—even now, at a funeral or at a friend's nuptials, praying in muffled tones and shooting side-glances at spirit-filled neighbors in the pew lifting their hearts and souls to the Lord in unself-conscious hosanna glory! I haven't attended mass regularly since I was in my late teens, and what's driven me back into church the several odd if intense times was the need to run away from myself, that desire itself feeling more and more as the preening of egotism. Only now am I lifting my head and wondering what it is I'm galloping toward. Or asking for.

The Alphabet in the Shag Carpet

Each summer when I was young my family rented a house at Bethany Beach, in Delaware. The drive along Route 50 from suburban Washington D.C., east across Maryland, over the vaulting span of the Chesapeake Bay Bridge, and through the choked, rural towns of Delaware: the eyes-closed fears crossing the bridge, staving off images of our station wagon plummeting into the Bay (worse returning home, when we'd cross at night through black so dark the water could've been miles, inches away); the dry farm towns so quiet and queer beyond tree-and-curb suburbia; the rising smell of the salt air as we got closer to the shore and the end of the country.

Leaving our rented house to go to the beach for the day, I saw a dead bird on the driveway, its wings fresh and glistening. For a week I walked past the bird, early in the dewy mornings and late in the sun-burned afternoons, and each day the body turned out a little more, decaying, welcoming flies, then maggots, then air, reducing as something nameless moved in. The seven-day death march was odd and agonizing, as the bird carcass played out in public its private, humiliating dissolve. I squeaked by in sneakers, clutching a beach towel.

This Must Be Where My Obsession With Infinity Began

My older brothers and sister walked by, disinterested. I had nothing to say about it, no one to say it to.

Later that week at Funland in Rehoboth Beach, the Atlantic behind me vanishing into the dark in its exhilarating, terrifying way. I'm eleven or twelve, heady in the salty, cotton-candy, blacktop-tar night and the roar of unseen waves at my back. Around me boys play with invisible-dog leashes, and girls with soda-red mouths wear Led Zeppelin shirts, perched shyly next to rail-thin guys with bare chests and tans and everybody's hair is shaggy and bleached — but I'm watching my dad and younger brother on the helicopter ride. The kiddie copters go around and around, one of my favorite rides. The best part was the metal bar across your lap that you lift you to make the copter fly up; push the bar down and the copter gently descends, a thrill in my chest every time. I'm watching my dad and my brother, waiting my turn, but their copter isn't rising or dropping, it flies steady in a cheerless, straight line. Other copters float and sink around them, and the kids' mouths are open and gleeful while my brother is pushing at the bar, his face clouding over. As my dad catches my eye and shrugs his shoulders, my brother's face turns red. Their copter passes by me, and my dad looks feeble. [And here I would insert the right word, if it existed, for tenderness, defeat, minor grief.]

I'm with a friend in his bedroom at the end of the summer. We're playing on the floor with cards, and something happens and very quickly he gets upset and makes fists with his sweaty hands and screws his legs into the ground, his breathing coming in bursts and gasps — then he remembers something and takes off for the living room. He slides to his knees into the shag carpeting and starts scrawling shapes with his index finger, a smile tracing its way onto his face as he breathes a little more deeply. *What are ya doing? I ask. My mom said when I feel real mad like I'm gonna yell or punch something or something to take a deep breath and write the alphabet into the carpet* and I look down and watch as the letters materialize, a jumble of words that make sentences that one day might name the weird anger that dropped this kid to his knees.

This Must Be Where My Obsession With Infinity Began

Into The Fable

Outdoors Day: the annual Spring afternoon away from the stuffy classrooms and onto the track and ball fields, dreaded by nearly all underclassmen save for the dozen or so who savored a May ritual of barely-disguised competition. We ran, we threw, we jumped. We "got some exercise," the athletically-challenged of us huffing and dripping awkwardly in the sun.

John D., doughy, soft in the hips, would rather have spent the afternoon in biology lab. He arrived limping into the school parking lot at eight a.m. sharp, injured by a rock discharged from the lawn mower he'd pushed through his family's yard. He exaggerated his sore ankle, shifting from leg to leg, and his face—normally pinkish, as if a mild sunburn had taken permanent place—blazed with discomfort. We teased him from the start. Quaking, he pleaded his case repeatedly but was never believed. The coincidence of having injured himself the day before Outdoors Day? Too much. Hoots and jeers drowned out his protestations for the rest of the banal afternoon. Poor John. Despite friendly times he and I shared in class and in the hallway, his face is locked

This Must Be Where My Obsession With Infinity Began

in that excruciating moment common to adolescence: caught in a lie, a public revision of history that the next twenty-four hours (a lifetime in one's mid-teens) a little maturity, a little self-esteem might have rendered obsolete.

Looking back, what remains speaks to randomness or to some sort of higher if obscure plan. That which we prize as the truth, we carry away from the stream dark and treasured in our pockets and caress, or try and crush, or buff unconsciously until it resembles something believable, understandable, comprehensible. That John's particular minor fabrication has lingered in my mind for decades begs me to trust it as some sort of enlightened moment. I know why he woke up and planned the fake limp; I want to know why I can't shake it. John has entered the fable. He's become a literary figure. He's become fabled. Does that mean that I invented him? He's now fabulous. He's now somewhere, not thinking of me.

But there he is, skulking around the perimeters of the track, kicking pebbles, alone, an hourglass Greek body hunched in the inescapable truth. He blew it; the lie didn't take. I could have done the same thing. Somewhere in the present tense of the past John's savoring the irony of injuring his ankle the day before certain athletic shame, or he's limping away from some kind of candor. Into the fable he goes.

Gone

Opening: *a white suburban house, sharp focus, medium shot, no sound. An establishing shot. Establishing what? The camera overcranks. Roll focus: a small child, evidently tossed into the air, slowly rises from the bottom frame. His feet glide upwards as his body comes to rest mid-frame. There's a look on his face you've seen before. His shoe laces stretch toward a clear sky, defying gravity for the moment. One soft, out-turned pocket floats. Gently, he begins to drop. He disappears quietly beneath the frame. Roll focus: the house, which appears quiet. Several seconds pass. Roll focus: a small girl floats upward from the bottom frame. Her eyes are shut tight, her body fetal. She glides upward, softly, as in a dream. Softly, she falls. She disappears beneath the frame. The house remains unfocused in the background. After several seconds the boy reappears from the bottom frame, gently rising. Just as slowly, he falls.*

For many years I've experienced two recurring images in my mind's-eye, not dreams but wakeful phantasms. One image is actually a pair of images: apropos of nothing—I could be reading, driving, listening to music—I'm faced with the

This Must Be Where My Obsession With Infinity Began

image of a great jet airliner's tail wing covered with charcoal-black graffiti, the precise words obscured. After a moment it is replaced by a long shot of an indeterminate black car—usually it's an old Volkswagen bug—half-covered in freshly-fallen snow, resting quietly on a frozen lake. Just as quickly the images vanish. Occasionally they switch positions, but always they come paired, two sides of a confounding riddle.

Another unbidden image. This one originates from an old dream. At the end of this dream—the rest of which I have forgotten—I stand in the parking lot of Saint Andrew the Apostle grade school as my younger brother (who, although he's three years younger than I am, appears in my dreams exclusively as a kid) is being driven away from me in a yellow school bus, his sad, round face pressed up against the last window.

My brother and I never rode school busses. Nor have I ever seen a graffitied jet wing. But these images are now hard-wired in me, as integral as DNA, as complex, as mysterious, as oddly necessary. I guess that they'll accompany me for the rest of my life, a kind of sign language that I blink at as a lost foreigner. Still, they repeat.

When I was six years old I had my adenoids removed at Holy Cross Hospital. Once, passing by a room, I glanced in to see a small boy my age sitting in a wheelchair, grinning. His head was shaved and his skull was punctured by a dozen tiny, black holes.

He visited again last night. When we are tapped on the shoulder we wheel around but stare at a gaping field. Longingly, we look to the ground for prints.

Jackie was an ugly girl. At age twelve, I could see it: the

doughy, mottled face, the bulbous and hooked nose, the fat legs, the stringy hair. I confidently assumed the general playground condemnation of her, joined in the ranks of those who intuited, somehow, that she was less fortunate than the rest of us. I posses an image of Jackie jauntily swinging her red backpack as she crosses the blacktop toward Saint Andrew's, dumbly eager to ignore what her stocky body bears all too heavily. My memory fades, or the frame snaps, before Jackie nears anyone on the blacktop who might skip toward her in blithe, giddy friendship, thrusting out a girlish embrace. Were I to somehow unearth this lost footage of my memory, and thread the dusty film gingerly through a projector, I might watch as Jackie walks alone toward a home I often wondered about.

She was the predictable brunt of jokes. Once in the cafeteria, Andy asked her to a dance and we all watched the charade, smothering snorts and giggles behind our hands. When the reality dawned on her, Jackie's face drained of color and her mouth dropped open as if she were puzzling over a problem that everyone else had solved. There were no friends for her to dash away with. Instead, she bore it up; I distinctly remember her back stiffening beneath her white uniform blouse. Whether she turned on her heel and left, or stayed and stomached her lunch beneath the hoots, I can't recall. At an all-school picnic in Rock Creek Park, Jenny, a very pretty blonde girl recently stripped of popular status, and so reduced to making friends with the likes of Jackie, told everyone she could a sad and juicy truth: *Jackie told me last night that her dad comes home with liquor on his breath!*

The drama of this public cruelty had a more complex timbre for us. This gossip reeked of home, of privacy, of desperate confidences. This joke made my small chest go cold. Jackie's humiliations were dragged from her house, her privacy pawed at and scattered. We had thoroughly defeated her now.

(How clichéd this all sounds! The lonely homely girl, the alcoholic father, the unthinking, opportunistic classmates. I hesitate as I write about Jackie's misfortunes: clichés arise from truth, of course, though their dailiness obscures and undermines truth-telling. The sharing of such childish cruelties morphs into a kind of adolescent pornography; sheer repetition of a stock narrative numbs us. And yet it lingers, like a mother's tight grip, leaving a mark. Jackie's complicated face in the cafeteria, her audible gasp as Jenny gleefully cried out her secrets. A bruise remains.)

So much has changed from my youth. The woods remain fecund, though they have mostly vanished. When I visit my parents' house in Wheaton, Maryland, the house in which I was raised, I remember the alarming rate at which nearby woods were removed when I was a kid. Woods wherein I once lost myself in heady darkness were leveled with astonishing ease and alacrity, paved for handsome, large, bright houses with forbidding doors and enormous picture windows. Equally curious were the changes going on in the back yard of Dr. and Mrs. Fox, who lived in the house directly next to our split-level on Amherst Avenue. The house had long since made its presence felt as a chalky white acid seeping beneath the north fence that bordered our yard, choking off an increasingly widening circle of our grass. I remember my mom peering down at the mysterious patch one afternoon with discreet consternation, behaving as the trained nurse she was. To me it seemed as if our neighbors were simply more advanced than we were. After all, they had a pool in their backyard—we did not, we never would—and surely our creeping glacier was small if inevitable price to pay for their suburban enhancement. Less wilderness to mow.

As the natural world slowly vanished, I lost a kind of enchantment. I looked forward to the end of my daily walk home from Saint Andrew's: a diversion through Mr. and Mrs. Vengrouskie's backyard on Arcola Avenue. A tiny creek zigzagged through their property over which they had constructed a small footbridge made of quartz- and mica-rocks and concrete. This blessed their yard with a nearly European, old-world charm to my ten-year-old self, and I'd make believe that I was in the Black Forest in Germany, with miles of hills and solitude and friendly, pie-faced children awaiting me when I emerged. The tiny bridge led me into the recesses of the Vengrouskie's yard, perpetually cool even on the most humid of suburban Washington D.C. afternoons, a darkly draped mini-forest that, though it was merely a hundred or so feet from my own home, transported me. The Vengrouskie's modest, landscaped yard bordered a larger woods that my friend Mike had the great fortune of living next to. In fact, for many years—until they were leveled for a large house—these woods were his backyard. We would lose ourselves in the maze of thickly-growing ash, acorn, and maple trees, navigating a course of fallen limbs and dive-bombing crows. The moment I entered these woods, my sense of demarcation—the civic parlance of suburbia—lifted. This must be where my obsession with infinity began.

My sensuality began to bloom as well, though dimly. Years after these tress were razed I kept a pornographic novel hidden in the moist recesses of a tree stump across the street from my house. By the time I'd reach it each day—and it was all that I could think to do—my heart would be pounding up through my neck, my hormonal body trusting to fear and lurid excitement. Lifting the book from the stump was a nearly obscene gesture: the novel was often heavy with the prior evening's rainfall, and I'd gently pick away slugs and snails from the cover to reveal the nude, languorous woman pictured there. The damp and crass knowledge inside was fiercely erotic, and sprang from the fecund wetness all around me, the sharp, pungent odor of sopping grass and dank trees. It was a drizzling kind of erotics. My hands literally trembled as I peeled pages apart like layers of skin.

Years earlier, the woods behind the Mike's house was the scene of an event that remains troubling in my imagination. Predictably, details refuse to marshal and present themselves: I'm sure of the participants, but wildly unsure of the particulars. What year? What season? What motives? Mike was always a risky boy, the kind who, when dared, would eat gum off of the street. His face seemed perpetually smudged with dirt and mischief. He wore a sandy-hair bowl cut and a crooked grin that stretched out devilishly beneath a freckled nose. He was slightly older than I, so stood as a kind of talisman of life's scary, sensational possibilities.

He had a younger sister named Lori who was playing with us in the woods one afternoon. Lori was with us under protest, and I remember her whimperings and objections. Some generalities of an ordinary afternoon: Mike slightly taller than I, and smirking; Lori, tiny and foal-like, trembling; me, witness. Mike held a black magic-marker in his hand and yanked down Lori's shorts after she had refused, in a desperately squirming kind of way, to undress for us. I remember Mike bending his little sister over a tree stump and scrawling a word with that pen onto her.

Gone

How often we gravitate toward the magnetic comforts of narrative as we assemble and reassemble the machinery of our lives. Details seem to fall into place, but I don't know if they're valid details or a kind of fictional integrity, components of the pleasure-seeking impulse to shape a story into order, and order into a kind of knowledge. The great fear that leans over my life like a verdict is that *I made it all up*. Did I dream such awful transgression in the woods? I could track down the rumor, the possibility, the wishes, see what leads me to the truth of Jackie alone on the playground. But my sad dreams of Jackie's house might not have been validated had I met her father, her mother, peered into her bedroom, a haunt of misery. Her face and her facts linger in the shimmering that encircles her, the gloomy atmosphere through which she sifts.

So much of the world blurs. I remember Mr. Vengrouskie slimming year after year as he walked past our house. I'd watch everyday as he strolled south along Amherst Avenue, ambling past our large kitchen window, a small, brown sack of sunflower seeds in his palm. He walked and chewed, walked and chewed for years, it seemed, his fat, round body slowly slipping away, until in the final months he was nothing more than some fused rails bound up in baggy pants. Only recently I learned that he was a town drunk, that he was walking— every day of my childhood—to Rosie's, the old-man bar three blocks down the road, a narrow train-car of gloom into which I'd occasionally peer during my allowance walks. Dusty sun strained and leaned into the bar when the door was propped open, bathing hunched, toothless men in undershirts. Did they call me in? Only in my excitable fears. Before I knew dread I understood Mr. Vengrouskie's weight loss as the result of healthy constitutionals, renewed discipline,

This Must Be Where My Obsession With Infinity Began

a kind of hale self-control. But he was wasting away at the bar, outside of a vexed marriage, and, later, by ravaging cancers. The stroll past my house brought him from point Z to point Z. He emerged from the woods behind his house as a kind of truth, one that I assembled over many years, but the truth was myth, a wished-for story. He emerged from the woods and the woods began disappearing behind him, met by machines that condensed them efficiently one row at a time, renewed them with domesticated tree houses that promised stories that could be told and trusted, known and embraced. As the woods vanished, so did those other stories, those whispered and dubious stories, unknown and avoided, leaving sticky tracks of desire, or flickering like bright images in a grove of trees.

I don't remember what word Mike wrote in big block letters onto his sister. All I remember is her hot, feverish tears and the image of her dashing home, struggling to pull up her shorts. What was that word? A curse we'd recently learned on the playground? Something vulgar and sexist, or scatological? Stare now as I might at the memory of Lori's tiny body, I cannot will the word to appear. Like all words, this was subsumed into the grandeur of language itself. What remains is a gesture, the music of defacement. Mike inscribing his sister's body was language asserting itself in the worst kind of way. The degree to which I am plagued by the shadowy details is language asserting differently, a beckoning toward some kind of understanding.

And why do I remember that Mike chose to write a single word? Why not a goofy face? A caricature of President Nixon? A ruthless squiggle, even. But a single word? Like my visiting jet wing covered in graffiti, the specific language remains blurry. All that remains is language. Mike, a crude linguist, was laying claim on his younger sister, branding her in his own idiom. Lori squirming, the lurid shock of her bright white body in the woods. The world suddenly privatized itself, and the three of us shared an intimacy, morally dubious and humiliating, in those few moments.

Language slips from us, resisting the simple categories that our scrapbooks demand. Words, images lurk in us as an approaching storm that promises a downpour but never arrives. They're the riddles that we create our personalities by, and a search for answers helps to assemble the stuff of our humanity. In childhood, the struggle begins to match language to deed, but as the woods around me were lifted and lain as so many tamed logs onto the back of trucks, spirited down the road into weakening daylight, so has the language of our youth faded, words once tremblingly composed to allow meaning its ache in our throats. Jackie whispered her secrets to Jenny in dogged vulnerability, Mike printed a word on his sister's sex, I sift for sense.

Faces flow in and out of memory, the pallid images. Children learn geometry the hard way, when the infinite world gapes open before them, or mysterious enemies leap from out of dark corners. One of the numerous tricks that memory plays on us is to elasticize space: when I enter a new building for the first time, I have an inflated feel for dimensions; I visit the building regularly and its size reduces properly. The imagination, when it encounters fresh space, searches for the infinite—this seems to me as fundamental to the human condition as anything else. Orwell knew it, so does that kid in the yard there. Similarly, when I revisit a building from my youth its dwarfish dimensions surprise me, as if an entire story or wing has vanished: when I walked through the halls of Saint Andrew's recently I felt as if I were in a doll's house. The root of the word *art* is *ar*: "to put together." Confounding language! How can I assemble a story when the parts keep stretching and reducing in size? It's difficult to trust such a surrealist blueprint. Memory's proportions bedevil my desk, swept clean in an attempt to put together the past.

This Must Be Where My Obsession With Infinity Began

Acknowledgements

I'm grateful to the editors at the following journals where these essays first appeared, some in different form: *Bellingham Review* ("Drafting The Beast"); *Brevity* ("Cathy Or Katy," "Into The Fable"); *Caketrain* ("On Gazing"); *Center: A Journal of the Literary Arts* ("Colonizing The Past"); *Cimarron Review* ("Bob's Blues"); *Connotation Press* ("The Alphabet In The Shag Carpet"); *Denver Quarterly* ("Acting Lessons"); *DIAGRAM* ("This Exhalation," "Yard Trauma"); *EUCALYPTUS* ("Customized Environmental Sound Machine"); *Faultline* ("Suburban Abstract"); *The Fiddleback* ("There Was The Occasional Disruption"); *Fourth Genre* ("Occasional Prayer"); *Hotel Amerika* ("One Halloween," "The Sky's Tent"); *Lofty Ambitions* ("Abstracting My Dad"); *New Ohio Review* ("The God-Blurred World"); *nidus* ("Student Killed By Freight Train"); *The Normal School* ("Gone"); *Poetry Northwest* ("After Serving," "The Innocents"); *Quarter After Eight* ("Exegesis" [as "Notes for a Narrative"], "Throwing Stones At Mina," "After Cornell"); *Quarterly West* ("Lime Green"); *River Teeth* ("Swooning At Saint Andrew's," "Caught"); *Seneca Review* ("Transparencies"); *Sonora Review* ("Spying On The Petries");

This Must Be Where My Obsession With Infinity Began

Southwest Review ("Trains And Ties" [as "Reflections On Trains And Ties"]); *Sou'wester* ("Fragments Of Terrain"); *Storyscape* ("The Magicians"); *Under the Sun* ("Looking For Karl"); *Waccamaw* ("The Blur Family"); *The Westminster Review* ("9th Street," "Stories")

"Exegesis" (as "Notes for a Narrative") also appeared in *The Next Of Us Is About To Be Born: Wick Poetry Series Anthology* (Kent State University Press). "After Serving" also appeared in *The Rose Metal Press Field Guide to Prose Poetry: Contemporary Poets in Discussion and Practice* (Rose Metal Press)

ABOUT THE AUTHOR

Joe Bonomo's essays and prose poems have appeared in numerous journals, magazines, and anthologies. A celebrated music writer, his books include *Conversations With Greil Marcus, AC/DC's Highway to Hell* (33 1/3 Series), *Jerry Lee Lewis: Lost and Found,* and *Sweat: The Story of the Fleshtones, America's Garage Band.* He teaches at Northern Illinois University and appears online at *No Such Thing As Was.*